D1150285

Contents

NOTES

Introduction

The publication of *Jane Eyre* on 16th October 1847 was a milestone in the history of the English novel. An instant popular success, it was reviewed in countless magazines and journals, and everywhere praised for its exceptional originality and riveting power.

> This is not only a work of great promise; it is one of absolute performance. It is one of the most powerful domestic romances which have been published for years. It has little or nothing of the old conventional stamp upon it; none of the jaded, exhausted attributes of a worn-out vein of imagination... but is full of youthful vigour, of freshness and originality... It is a book to make the pulses gallop and the heart beat, and to fill the eyes with tears. (Anonymous reviewer in the *Atlas*, 23rd October 1847)

Jane Eyre's success owed a lot to its timing: "Brontë's first novel made its appearance in the somewhat dismal interval between, on the one hand, Jane Austen and Scott, and, on the other, the most eventful period in the novel's history," wrote the critic Miriam Allott. Yet more than 150 years later, it still powerfully affects its readers with all the charge of a new-minted work. "Read by thousands who have no idea of its period, who devour it unaware of difficulties, unconscious of any need for adaptation to unfamiliar manners or conventions, *Jane Eyre* makes its appeal first and last to 'the unchanging human heart'," said Kathleen Tillotson.

It is easy to forget, now, how shocking the novel was to its mid-19th century readers. Virtually every early reviewer felt obliged either to condemn or defend its impropriety. The most savage reviews denounced the "coarseness" of language, the "unfeminine" laxity of moral tone, and the "dereliction of decorum" which made its hero cruel, brutal, yet attractively interesting, while permitting its plain, poor, single heroine to live under same roof as the man she loved. What caused most outrage, perhaps, was the demonstrable rebellious anger in the heroine's "unregenerate and undisciplined spirit", her being a passionate law unto herself. "Never was there a better hater. Every page burns with moral Jacobinism," wrote an early critic. As the poet Matthew Arnold was to say of Brontë's "disagreeable" final novel, *Villette*, "the writer's mind contains nothing but hunger, rebellion and rage".

Though the view of the novel as "anti-Christian" was extreme, many readers criticised its melodrama, improbability and unnatural artifice. For most, though (then as now), these flaws are not only entirely explicable in view of the writer's youth but are amply compensated for by Brontë's intellectual seriousness, moral integrity and depth of feeling.

> Reality – deep, significant reality – is the great characteristic of the book. It is an autobiography, – not, perhaps, in the naked facts and circumstances, but in the actual suffering and experience... It is soul speaking to soul; it is an utterance from the depths of a struggling, suffering, much-enduring spirit. (George Henry Lewes, December 1847)

For all its compelling love interest, it is worth recalling that *Jane Eyre* was regarded even by the Romantic sensibility of late 19th-century poet Algernon Charles Swinburne as a work of "genius" first and foremost because of its realism:

> The gift of which I would speak is that of a power to make us feel in every nerve, at every step forward... thus and not otherwise... it was and must have been with the human figures set before us in their action and their suffering; that thus and not otherwise they absolutely must and would have felt, thought and spoken.

A summary of the plot

The novel opens at Gateshead Hall where orphaned 10-year-old Jane is the adopted child of her Aunt Reed. Neglected and emotionally rejected by her aunt, Jane is cruelly treated by her cousins, Eliza, Georgiana, and John, especially the latter. After one incident, where Jane uncharacteristically retaliates, she is locked in the red room in which her Uncle Reed had died and suffers terrifying delusions. Soon afterwards, Jane is sent to the charitable institution, Lowood School, where the director, to whom Mrs Reed has unfairly denounced Jane as deceitful, submits her to the public humiliation of being branded a liar. The tyranny of the school's regime is relieved for Jane by the friendship of Helen Burns – whose death from consumption is a direct result of the appalling conditions at the school – and the mentorship of the school's superintendent, Miss Temple.

After eight years as both pupil and teacher at Lowood, Jane accepts a post as governess at Thornfield Hall. Before leaving Lowood, she is informed by the Gateshead servant, Bessie, that her other uncle, John Reed, has been seeking her. At Thornfield, Jane's pupil is Adèle, ward of the absent master, Rochester. Before Rochester's return, Jane hears strange laughter as she wanders the third storey of the mansion and is informed that the laughter is that of a servant, Grace Poole. Walking out one winter's day, Jane unwittingly comes to the aid of Rochester when he falls from his horse. Rochester is drawn to Jane, seeks her companionship, and the two become passionately close. Rochester confesses to a sinful history of sexual indiscretion, including his affair with French mistress Céline Varens, of which liaison Adèle is apparently the offspring. That same night, Jane is disturbed by the strange "demoniac" laughter and by smoke issuing from Rochester's bedchamber. She finds Rochester asleep, his bed aflame, and douses the fire. He thanks her for saving his life, addressing her as his "cherished preserver".

Following an unannounced absence of several weeks, Rochester returns to Thornfield with house guests who include Blanche Ingram, whom, to all appearances, Rochester is wooing and intends to marry. During the house party, Rochester disguises himself as a fortune-telling gypsy and uses this cover, which Jane eventually sees through, to probe Jane's feelings as well as to disabuse Blanche Ingram of her notions of his wealth. That night the household is disturbed by the violent attack, accompanied by a savage cry, upon a visitor to Thornfield, Richard Mason. As Jane tends Mason's wounds at Rochester's request while he seeks medical help, she hears wild animal snarls in the room her patient has come from. Mason leaves Thornfield directly and Jane is herself recalled to Gateshead by the dying Mrs Reed, who wishes to confess to Jane that, when Jane's uncle John had come in search of his niece to make her his heir, Mrs Reed had claimed that Jane was already dead.

When Jane returns to Thornfield, Rochester admits that his intentions toward Blanche Ingram were never serious, and proposes to Jane, who accepts. That night the chestnut tree under which they had been sitting is split by lightning . On the eve of the wedding, Jane is visited by a spectral woman who tears her bridal veil. At the wedding ceremony, Mason returns accompanied by a lawyer who declares the intended marriage is invalid as Rochester is already married. Rochester takes the guests to his living wife – Mason's sister, the mad Bertha, who inhabits the third storey like a caged wild animal, and immediately attacks her husband. Rochester tries to persuade Jane to live as his mistress, but she refuses, and leaves Thornfield in the dead of night, destitute.

Wandering miles without shelter or food and close to death, Jane is taken in by the Rivers family at Marsh End, where she assumes a false name and begins in the lowly post of village school teacher offered to her by John Rivers. When John discovers her true identity, he realises that she is the unknown relation to whom his deceased uncle John Reed left his fortune, and that Jane is his cousin. Jane shares her inheritance with her cousins, but resists John's insistent request that she join him as his missionary wife in India. On the point of accepting, despite her reluctance, she hears Rochester's voice calling her name. Returning at once to Thornfield, she finds a burned-out ruin, set alight, she learns, by Bertha, who died in the flames, though not before Rochester had lost a hand and the sight of one eye in trying to save her. Jane finds Rochester at Ferndean, and the couple marry.

What is *Jane Eyre* about?

In outline, *Jane Eyre* is a love story; a Cinderella fable, depicting the transformation from forlorn, neglected childhood to happy, prosperous marriage; the ancient story of thwarted lovers who overcome obstacles and are finally united. Yet *Jane Eyre* interrogates, at every turn, the archetypes upon which it rests, especially, perhaps, the archetype Brontë inherited from her immediate literary forebear, Jane Austen. It is not simply that Jane is not pretty, humble or submissive, nor that her lover, Rochester, is not young, handsome or chivalrous. Though the couple's enduring sympathetic appeal against the grain of these conventional merits remains a *tour de force*, Jane Austen's heroines had already broken that mould.

The key difference is that, where sensual love is morally suspect and dangerous in Austen, in *Jane Eyre* it is a potential force for mutual good and growth as much as it is a catalyst for despair. Love, even when wildly and deliriously exciting, is not merely seductively pleasurable; nor is it benignly bountiful either. It is anger, jealousy, sex, joy, fear, desire, longing, pain, friendship, loss: its ground is moral, metaphysical and cosmic, as much as it is personal and carnal. It is as deeply satisfying as it is apparently incapable of offering the fulfilment of peace and serenity.

The difference between Austen's and Brontë's ideas of love is almost synonymous with the distinction between 18th-century rationalism and 19th-century Romanticism. At one level, the authors represent sense versus sensibility, as Brontë herself recognised in her famous scathing attack on Austen's novels.

> She ruffles her reader by nothing vehement... the Passions are perfectly unknown to her... Her business is not half so much with the human heart as with the human eyes, mouth, hands and feet; what sees keenly, speaks aptly, moves flexibly, it suits her to study, but what throbs fast and full, though hidden, what the blood rushes

through, what is the unseen seat of Life... Miss
Austen ignores.

Yet it is as true for Brontë as for her literary *bête
noire* that, while a loving union with a fellow being
was the ultimate destiny, it was not the essential
one, precisely because, for all the differences in
their temperaments and situations, both writers
shared a fundamentally Christian outlook. Mid-
20th century criticism often rightly emphasised
the novel's religious dimension. Its "inclusiveness
and unity comes from Jane's spiritual growth... as
well as her emotional adventure", writes Kathleen
Tillotson. Each stage of her progress – childhood
at Gateshead, adolescence at Lowood School,
maturity at Thornfield and Marsh End, fulfilment
and marriage at Ferndean – is marked by a
spiritual suffering and renewal, which is finally
matched by Rochester's own: "I was forced to pass
through the valley of the shadow of death." The
issue was never whether Jane should have become
Rochester's mistress, argues Robert Martin, but
that of finding the right relationship with God.

> The test is to become worthy of love, not to take it
> on any terms but to deserve it: not to violate one's
> own nature and morality but so to expand that
> nature that it deserves reward. Jane and
> Rochester, learning to respect the inviolability of
> the soul as much as earthly delights, become a

microcosm of man's striving for Christian reward.

But as the seminal feminist reading by Sandra Gilbert and Susan Gubar in the 1980s pointed out, in borrowing from John Bunyan the mythic-spiritual quest narrative, *Jane Eyre* is a distinctively female *"Pilgrim's Progress"*: "the problems encountered by the protagonist as she struggles from the imprisonment of her childhood toward an almost unthinkable goal of mature freedom are symptomatic of difficulties Everywoman in a patriarchal society must meet and overcome: oppression (at Gateshead), starvation (at Lowood), madness (at Thornfield), and coldness (at Marsh End)". As the 19th-century novelist, Margaret Oliphant, more disparagingly put it in 1855, *Jane Eyre* represented "the new generation nailing its colours to the mast... this furious love-making was but a wild declaration of the 'Rights of Woman' in a new aspect".

Perhaps what finally holds together the Christian and feminist, spiritual and rebellious, subjective and social elements in *Jane Eyre* is its overwhelming commitment to depicting the struggle of an individual consciousness towards fulfilment, within and against the restraints which determine and shape an individual life, in homage to the author's Romantic forbears, Wordsworth, Coleridge and Byron:

[Charlotte Brontë] aimed at achieving through prose fiction something as serious, vital, and significant as the work of [her] favourite poets, which should voice the tragic experience of life, be true to the experience of the whole woman, and convey a sense of life's springs and undercurrents. To envisage such a possibility for the novel was at that date a critical achievement of the first order; to succeed... in carrying it out was proof of great creative genius... This effort in due course led to the novel's becoming the major art form of the nineteenth century. (Q. D. Leavis's Introduction to the 1966 Penguin edition)

What kind of novel is *Jane Eyre*?

The straightforward answer to this is a fictional autobiography. The closest match in Jane Eyre's own experience to Charlotte Brontë's is, famously, her early schooling. In 1824, Charlotte, aged eight, and Emily, aged six, joined their sisters Maria and Elizabeth at Cowan Bridge boarding school. There, they were subjected to a punishing regime of cold, hunger and ill-health, apparently based on evangelical principles of promoting spiritual regeneration through rigorously enforced discipline, but mostly the result of sheer negligence. The older sisters quickly succumbed to fatal tuberculosis, and further ill-treatment. "I need hardly say," said Elizabeth Gaskell, friend, fellow-novelist and biographer of Charlotte Brontë, "that Helen Burns is [an] exact transcript of Maria Brontë... [Charlotte's] heart, to the latest day on which we met, still beat with unavailing indignation at the worrying and the cruelty to which her gentle, patient, dying sister had been subjected."

If little else in *Jane Eyre* reflects so closely actual events, there are large portions of the novel in which biographical data is recast, purged or vicariously consummated. It is not simply the claim of myth or reductive caricature that the character of Rochester is an amalgam of the distinct and extreme personality types of the two men among her limited masculine acquaintance whom Charlotte knew intimately; and with whom, from childhood, she shared the kind of intellectually emotional openness and partnership which Brontë's heroines always seek, and prize more highly than conventional romantic love.

Her father, Patrick, was learned, intelligent, eccentric, dominant, while loving, caring and compassionate; her brother, Branwell, was gifted, self-absorbed, irresolutely ambitious, with a propensity for drink, depression and dissolution. Charlotte owed to her non-censorious father the liberal literary education (including the works of racy Byron and Shelley, generally regarded as unfit for Victorian female readership) which influenced her portrayal of Rochester, while Branwell's scandalous sexual indiscretions provided a real-life example of the Byronic hero. Moreover, while Charlotte was unequivocal in her contempt of Branwell's misconduct, she suffered, during the same period, her own secret and apparently unreturned passion for a married man,

THE CHILD IN VICTORIAN FICTION

Jane Eyre brings together in one heroine the two roles which arguably embodied most tension for 19th-century English society – the orphan child and the governess (see page 33) – and which, for that very reason, made them focal points of conflict and interrogation in Victorian fiction. *Jane Eyre* helped both to define and to problematise these traditions.

The generation of poets which preceded the Victorian period (in particular, Blake, Coleridge and Wordsworth) – influenced by Jean-Jacques Rousseau's *Émile or A Treatise on Education*, which seeks to show how natural human goodness can survive corrupt society – had established the child as the archetype of Romantic sensibility. The child represented individuality, innocence, imagination, heightened sensitivity and fragility, and could be as powerfully expressive of nostalgia and Wordsworthian "natural piety" as of Blakean indignant social protest.

One of Charles Dickens's

her Brussels schoolmaster, M. Heger, whose notice and admiration of her intellectual powers was one of the most significant events of her life. While this experience provided the undisputed template for Charlotte Brontë's later novel, *Villette*, the author's quasi-obsessive attachment also haunts the dynamic of separation and longing in the heroine's relationship with Rochester in *Jane Eyre*.

In one of the few studies really to consider the

major achievements was to place the Romantic child, for the first time, at the heart of the English novel – an essentially un-Romantic mode, whose form and medium was prosaic, and whose subject tended to be the grim reality of urban and industrial poverty. *Oliver Twist* (1838) was the first novel in English to focus on the child as its central interest. After that, over three decades (through *Dombey and Son*, *David Copperfield*, *Great Expectations* and *Bleak House*), a child's story – as neglected daughter, abused step-son, social-climber and orphaned street child, possessed of moral penetration and often mortal awareness – generates the emotional energy of Dickens's novels and exposes every imaginable social ill.

Jane Eyre stands alongside Dickens's work in establishing a new tradition in English fiction. Arguably, in fact, it exceeds Dickens's achievement by expressing the psychic condition of childhood deprivation and persecution – giving to the isolation and helplessness witnessed by Oliver Twist a depth of psychological perception and emotional realism which was without precedent. Peter Coveney writes: "Jane Eyre is perhaps the first heroine in English fiction to be given, chronologically at least, as a psychic whole. Nothing, in fact, quite like Jane Eyre had ever been attempted before." •

formal implications of the autobiographical dimension of Charlotte Brontë's fiction, Roy Pascal claims that even the "lies" are in the service of authenticity. "What Brontë sought to do, in altering circumstances and events" – especially, in substituting the fantasy of love-fulfilment for the rejection she herself had suffered – was not to find vicarious or compensatory satisfaction, but "to get nearer to the real truth of her own character, of its hidden capacities as well as its realised actuality... In this sense her novel is truer to her real character than life itself was, for it unfolds these resources which life seems determined to choke. Imagination has not distorted truth but shaped the shapeless."

Generically speaking, however, the fictional autobiography is almost inseparable from the 19th-century *Bildungsroman*, or novel of development, which traces the moral and psychological development of a single individual from childhood to adulthood. These two fictional modes "grew up" together in the Victorian period, and *Jane Eyre* is the most original and remarkable of its type (which includes Dickens's *David Copperfield* and *Great Expectations* and George Eliot's *The Mill on the Floss*) because it founded the female version of the genre. The first women's *Bildung*, by its very nature, could not help intersecting with every aspect of "the woman question" in the 19th century, and no novel

Poster for the French version of Robert Stevenson's 1943 film

displays better than this one how far down into individual female being the social and economic determinants of patriarchy can go:

> *Women are supposed to be very calm generally: but women feel just as men feel; they need exercise for their faculties, and a field for their efforts as much as their brothers do; they suffer from too rigid a restraint, too absolute a stagnation, precisely as men would suffer; and it is narrow-minded in their more privileged fellow-creatures to say that they ought to confine themselves to making puddings and knitting stockings, to playing on the piano and embroidering bags. It is thoughtless to condemn them, or laugh at them, if they seek to do more or learn more than custom has pronounced necessary for their sex. (12)**

But the radical individualism of *Jane Eyre* is arguably always more literary-philosophical than proto-feminist. The individual is not politically gendered but Romantically unique – the single self, prized and recognised, the more so for being socially diminished. "Nobody knows," Jane says in the same famous passage, "how many rebellions *besides political rebellions* ferment in the masses of life which people earth." In a period of British and European ferment and revolution, this

Throughout this book, the numbers in brackets refer to the chapters from which the quotations are taken.

sentence aligns Jane's internal struggles with those taking place contemporaneously in the socio-political domain. At the same time, it offers in miniature the mission of the book as a whole in its emphasis on the personal and inner life (especially female inwardness) rather than on the external pressures which help to shape it.

The novel itself, in other words, constituted female rebellion, not only in its boldly autobiographical Romantic expressionism (entirely new for a woman novelist), but in the way it incorporated standard elements of romance. While Brontë draws on the atmospherics of Gothic fiction to arouse mystery and intensify suspense, the novel's Gothic set pieces – the red room, the forbidden attic, the dangerously sexualised hero – are at once an imaginative carry-over from the childhood tales she composed with her siblings (Branwell especially) and an honouring of Byronic irrationalism and imaginative freedom. Both influences represent a refusal to bow to the respectably adult female domestic world and the fictional modes hitherto associated with it (Jane Austen's anti-Romantic rationalism in *Pride and Prejudice* at one extreme, Ann Radcliffe's female Gothic in *The Mysteries of Udolpho* at the other). The novel "manages to make Gothic more than a stereotype", says Robert B. Heilman, by finding new ways to achieve the ends served by old Gothic – the discovery and release of new patterns of feeling... rather than the exercise of old ones. *Jane Eyre's* "new Gothic" leads away from standardised characterisation towards new levels of human reality, and hence from stock responses towards a new kind of passionate engagement.

But even as the novel exploits and modifies Gothic conventions, it also parodies them in an anti-Gothic manner reminiscent of the author Brontë herself most disparaged – Jane Austen, in *Northanger Abbey*. The horrific scene in which Rochester's bed is aflame is daringly inflected with comedy when the hero curses the cold water which he finds Jane has poured over him; the description of the Ingram and Eshton house guests at Thornfield is an extended ironic treatment of social manners in the high style.

What kind of heroine is Jane Eyre?

Early in Chapter One, the son and heir of the family in which Jane is growing up, John Reed, bullies Jane into recognition of her subordinate position in the household. "You are a dependant...

you have no money, your father left you none; you ought to beg, and not to live here with gentlemen's children like us, and eat the same meals we do, and wear clothes at our mama's expense." Jane's demeanour of "habitual obedience" – "Accustomed to John Reed's abuse, I never had an idea of replying to it" – apparently casts her at the outset as the type of impoverished heroine of a traditional fairy-tale who meekly accepts her fate to be finally rewarded for her humility with happiness and love.

The words which begin Chapter Two, however, when Jane is being taken to the red room to be locked up – "I resisted all the way: a new thing for me" – break the traditional mould for a female heroine and initiate a radical new departure for the 19th-century novel. Jane's unique novelty as a heroine is that she does not – and increasingly will not – fit the female roles conventionally assigned to her, either social or literary. When Mrs Reed asserts to John that Jane is "not worthy of notice... [n]either you [n]or your sisters should associate with her", Jane's reaction is not dutifully submissive but instinctively and immediately retaliatory in counter-assertion of her own worth: "I cried out suddenly and without at all deliberating on my words, 'They are not fit to associate with me'" (4).

When Mrs Reed later denounces Jane to her future headmaster, Mr Brocklehurst, and Jane responds – "Speak I must: I had been trodden on severely and must turn" (4) – it is as though characteristically silenced, marginalised or ignored female experience – "bad feelings", "antagonistic energies", "fierce speaking" – is thus suddenly and dramatically vocalised. For the first time, the heroine's resistant voice is neither movingly pitiable, as with Shakespeare's Cordelia, nor winningly attractive or exemplarily moral, as with Jane Austen's Emma Woodehouse or Fanny Price.

READER, I...

The frequent instances of direct address to the reader in *Jane Eyre* have excited opposing critical responses. For some readers these instances are evidence of the author's consciousness that the novel's subject and language went against the conventional grain and represent special pleading for the reader's sympathy and, in Karl Kroeber's words, an attempt to "assert a community". For others, these interpolations are part of the novel's structure of growth, reminding us that the Jane who narrates her story is not identical with the Jane who experiences it, and suggesting that the reader is invited to share only in retrospection.

In addition, argues Karen Chase, "by reminding us so frequently of the narrative act, by calling us away from the recorded events to the reader/ writer relationship, [they] inevitably place us at one remove from these events". For

In fact, Jane's explicit acts of rebellion are foreshadowed at the outset. The opening of Chapter One describes Mrs Reed, "with her darlings about her", justifying her punitive orientation towards her charge:

Me, she had dispensed from joining the group; saying, "She regretted to be under the necessity of keeping me at a distance; but that until... I was endeavouring in good earnest to acquire a more sociable and child - like disposition, a more

other critics, like Jeanette King, the addressing voice varies with the occasion of its usage. While often, says King, "these apostrophes... share a confidence or feeling that Jane... is unable to express to any character in the novel... inviting intimacy between reader and *narrated* Jane" – a view which is cognisant of how little hindsight is exercised by the narrator – these interpolations also occur "at moments of heightened emotion, recalling us from the emotional past to the present of the narrating [and] increase in frequency as the narrated Jane gets older, closer in time to the narrator, drawing the reader's attention to the *distinction* as they appear to be on the point of merging".

The apparent openness of the narrator is also a kind of defensive strategy, such readings suggest. Perhaps these considerations are related to the author-narrator's tendency towards inverted syntax (pointed out by one of Brontë's biographers, Margot Peters), where the "I" (or its surrogates – "Reason", "Jane Eyre" – often rhetorically associated with the "Reader, I" formulation) emerges to bury a deeper self that exists beneath or inside the habitual social self or role the narrator is constrained to inhabit •

attractive and sprightly manner, – something
lighter, franker, more natural as it were – she
really must exclude me from privileges intended
only for contented, happy little children." (1)

The novel immediately invokes the conventions of
Victorian girlhood which this heroine, as we have
seen, apparently exists to oppose. Not only is
Jane a "parentless infant" and subordinate: she is
inferior in her size and the appeal of her looks as
well as in her status. She is "a discord" and that
very discordancy is almost defiantly present in the
first-person narration here. First, the proposed
ideal of female childhood is mediated entirely
through Jane's ironic consciousness of Mrs Reed's
reported words, not through direct dialogue.
Second, the syntax is itself ostentatiously
unorthodox. That prominent initial first-person
pronoun – "Me" – is positioned in silently
vengeful opposition to the family's will to dispense
with and ignore her.

Even so, Jane's rebellions are still
characteristically hidden and inward. The entire
red room episode is dramatic testimony to the
power of her imaginative life, which, even with its
terrorising facility, offers a retreat and a resource.
Reading Bewick's *History of British Birds*, Jane
finds herself singularly "happy":

Each picture told a story: mysterious often to my

undeveloped understanding... shadowy, like all the
half-comprehended notions that float dim through
children's brains, but strangely impressive. (1)

Such images seem distinctly Romantic and Jane's imaginative affinity with the natural world, together with her instinctively raw, innate, untrained sense of justice ("Unjust! unjust!" is Jane's inward cry at John Reed's "violent tyrannies") seems of a kind with the thinking of Rousseau and poets like Wordsworth and Coleridge. Indeed, the very genre of the *Bildungsroman* can be traced back to the influence of the Wordsworthian dictum that "the child is the father of the man" and the unprecedented interest in childhood as a formative and psycho-emotionally rich stage of life. For the first time, during the Romantic period, childhood was regarded not only as intrinsically significant as the foundation of subjectivity but as uniquely valuable for modelling natural innocence and goodness in a world of fallen experience.

Yet if Jane does not fit the ideal of conventional girlhood, neither does she readily fit the alternative Romantic paradigm. Her individual expressiveness, as we have seen, is closer in kind to Byronic rebellious energy and fierce opposition to constraint than it is to the Wordsworthian naturalist ideal. What is more, the first-person narration unobtrusively, if sympathetically, acknowledges the excessiveness of Jane's will to be "winner of the field" in "the hardest battle I had fought, and the first victory I had gained":

> "When I am grown up ... if anyone asks me how I liked you, and how you treated me, I will say the very thought of you makes me sick, and that you treated me with miserable cruelty."
>
> "How dare you affirm that, Jane Eyre?"
>
> "How dare I, Mrs Reed? How dare I? Because it is the truth."...
>
> Ere I had finished this reply, my soul began to expand, to exult, with the strangest sense of freedom, of triumph, I ever felt. It seemed as if an invisible bond had burst, and that I had struggled out into unhoped-for liberty... Mrs Reed looked frightened... Something of vengeance I had tasted for the first time; as aromatic wine it seemed on swallowing, warm and racy: its after-flavour, metallic and corroding, gave me a sensation as if I had been poisoned. (4)

This passage – and the whole scene from which it is excerpted – is a brilliant example of the novel's capacity for immersed absorption in the "*feel*" of childhood experience, its sensory primacy. As Jane herself says in Chapter Three, children "can feel, but they cannot analyse their feelings". Her angry words – "the very thought of you makes me sick" – are converted at the close, in part through the shocking visual perception of the result of the outburst – "Mrs Reed looked frightened" – into a virtual swallowing both of her own cruelty and of Mrs Reed's fear.

Readings of *Jane Eyre* which find in its heroine the definitive female version of the Romantic rebel against Victorian constraint neglect both the disturbingly visceral quality of this experience and its equivocal status within the novel. "When I am grown up" is a reminder not only of Jane's youth and immaturity but of how distant she is from the adult experience and understanding which inflects the first-person narration in these early chapters. "A child cannot quarrel with its elders, as I had done; cannot give its furious feelings uncontrolled play, as I had given mine; without experiencing afterwards the pang of remorse and the chill of reaction" (4). As Marianne Thormählen has pointed out in *The Brontës and Education*, "Charlotte's practical experiences of and with undisciplined children might have checked any inclination towards Rousseauan idealism, at least as regards child development".

But the double consciousness of this narrative discourse – adult perspective inflecting and interrogating a child's-eye view – is not, in *Jane Eyre*, rigidly reproving or moral. The gap between child and adult awareness is not didactically exploited as it is in *Great Expectations*: rather, the second layer of adult solicitude is protective, amending the vulnerable and bewildered shortfall in the child's vision:

> *How all my brain was in tumult, and all my heart in insurrection! Yet, in what darkness, what dense ignorance, was the mental battle fought! I could not answer the ceaseless inward question – why I thus suffered: now, at the distance of – I will not say how many years, I see it clearly... I was like nobody there; I had nothing in harmony with Mrs Reed or her children... a heterogeneous thing, opposed to them in temperament, in capacity, in propensities; a useless thing, incapable of serving their interest, or adding to their pleasure; a noxious thing, cherishing the germs of indignation at their treatment, of contempt of their judgment.* (2)

In such instances, the most illuminating comparison within 19th century fiction is not the reformed Pip but the uneducated, neglected and forgotten social "discord" of Dickens's *Bleak House*, the orphan child Jo. In place of Jo's "native ignorance" of the injustice he represents, we have a female articulate version of what that condition means *inwardly*.

What happens in the red room?

Jane's incarceration in the red room occupies only several pages of the book, but, like the window scene in which Catherine Earnshaw begs "Let me in – let me in" in Emily Brontë's *Wuthering Heights* – also centred on an excluded child figure – it is one of the most iconic moments in Victorian fiction, supercharged with a significance which haunts the remainder of the book.

> *The red room was a spare chamber, very seldom slept in... one of the largest and stateliest chambers in the mansion. A bed supported on massive pillars of mahogany, hung with curtains of deep red damask, stood out like a tabernacle in the centre; the two large windows, with their blinds always drawn down, were half shrouded in festoons and falls of similar drapery; the carpet was red; the table at the foot of the bed was covered with a crimson cloth; the walls were a soft fawn colour, with a blush of pink in it; the wardrobe, the toilet-table, the chairs were of darkly polished old mahogany. Out of these deep surrounding shades rose high, and glared white, the piled-up mattresses and pillows of the bed... Scarcely less prominent was an ample, cushioned easy-chair near the head of the bed, also white, with a footstool before it; and looking, as I thought, like a*

pale throne.

This room was chill... silent... solemn...

Mr Reed had been dead nine years: it was in this chamber he breathed his last; here he lay in state; hence his coffin was borne... and, since that day, a sense of dreary consecration had guarded it from frequent intrusion. (2)

This curiously understated and undramatic description has generated a rich afterlife of critical interpretation. The red room, say Gilbert and Gubar, "perfectly represents [Jane's] vision of the society in which she is trapped, an uneasy and elfin dependent":

> It is a kind of patriarchal death-chamber. The spirit of a society in which Jane has no clear place sharpens the angles of the furniture, enlarges the shadows, strengthens the locks on the door. And the deathbed of a father who is not really her father emphasises her isolation and vulnerability.

Jane's "Alas!... no jail was ever more secure" does indeed anticipate the forms of female imprisonment which dominate the book – her "boarding" at Lowood, the restricted field of effort to which she is "condemned" and, of course, Bertha's incarceration in the attic at Thornfield. The physical spaces of the novel are concrete images of female social oppression, where the experience of shut-in helplessness is a physical reality: "If you don't sit still, you must be tied down" (2). Gilbert and Gubar regard the red room as a paradigm not simply of inner female space but of the larger drama which occupies the entire book: Jane's anomalous position in society as orphan and governess, her enclosure in stultifying roles and houses, her attempts to escape through flight, starvation and madness.

Equally, however, the red room, like the other "female" spaces, is a compellingly interior space which not only frustratingly shuts out a larger world but encloses and dramatises an internal one. For John Maynard, the drama is essentially Oedipal. Jane is sent as punishment by the only official mother figure in her life (Mrs Reed, uncaring and hostile) to the one room which still recalls a loving parent figure, Jane's Uncle Reed. "Cold for all its warm colours because no fire is ever lit there", the room evokes "intense reminiscences of a loving relationship that only indicate to Jane the finality of her loss. Jane's experience of this room is essentially one of alienation. What should be a centre of warmth of affection is a place of cold and oppression."

For Elaine Showalter, the red room's "Freudian wealth of secret compartments, wardrobes, drawers, and jewel chest" gives it "strong associations with the adult female body" and Jane's "mad cat" behaviour stresses (as Bertha's will do, though more dramatically, later in the novel) "the fleshly aspects of adult female sexuality". For Sally Shuttleworth, too, the room's deadly and bloody connotations, and the flow of blood which marks Jane's entrance – "my head still ached and bled with the blow and fall I had received" – associate her confinement "with the onset of puberty" and the passage into womanhood. Moreover, Jane's experience captures the "bewildering, contradictory and polluting effects of suppression within the female frame" which help account for the curious episode of "alienated" dissociation when Jane catches sight of herself in the looking glass:

> *My fascinated glance involuntarily explored the depth it revealed. All looked colder and darker in that visionary hollow than in reality; and the strange little figure there gazing at me, with a white face and arms specking the glow, and glittering eyes of fear moving where all else was still, had the effect of a real spirit... [a] tiny phantom, half fairy, half imp. (2)*

For Helene Moglen, the coldly magnificent bedchamber, with its profound silence and sense of consecrated gloom is, at the same time – all the colour of blood, of fire, of passion – a kind of *birth* chamber. "It is a terrifying womb-world in which Jane loses her sense of the boundaries of identity, feels an inhabitant of another universe, and is thence born into a new state of being." The experience marks "the end of the submission of childhood and the beginning of a new stage of growth". Adrienne Rich similarly regards the episode as "the moment that the germ of the person we are finally to know as Jane Eyre is born; a person determined to live and to choose her life with dignity, integrity and pride":

My reason [was] forced by the agonising stimulus into precocious though transitory power; and Resolve, equally wrought up, instigated some strange expedient to achieve escape from insupportable oppression. (2)

But this "resolve", which is not itself free of fantasy – she thinks of "running away, or, if that could not be effected, never eating or drinking more, and letting myself die" (2) – is also accompanied by possibly the most traumatic vision in the book:

I doubted not – had never doubted – that if Mr Reed had been alive he would have treated me kindly... and I thought Mr Reed's spirit, harassed by the wrongs of his sister's child, might... rise before me in this chamber. I wiped my tears and hushed my sobs; fearful lest any sign of violent grief might waken a preternatural voice to comfort me... A light gleamed on the wall. Was it, I asked myself, a ray from the moon?... No; moonlight was still, and this stirred: while I gazed, it glided up to the ceiling and quivered over my head... I thought the swift-darting beam was a herald of some coming vision from another world. My heart beat thick, my head grew hot; a sound filled my ears, which I deemed the rushing of wings: something seemed near me; I was oppressed, suffocated: endurance broke down – I uttered a wild, involuntary cry... (2)

Jane's own wild cry directly anticipates the cry which will issue from Bertha's attic room at Thornfield (II, 5) and, earlier, at Jane's own chamber door (I, 15). Just so, the startling glimpse of a spirit face in the mirror will be repeated on the eve of Jane and Rochester's aborted wedding ceremony, when Jane will see in the glass not herself but Bertha – the first Mrs Rochester – wearing Jane's wedding veil as if in place of herself. The red room is also implicitly recalled when Jane is summoned to another masculine bedchamber – Rochester's – to find it terrifyingly red with real flame as a result of Bertha's setting it alight. The red room incident thus initiates the network of association which, as we shall see, holds Jane and Bertha both together and apart as twinned opposites of female adult being. "It functions as a kind of symbolic preface to the entire work," says John Maynard. Moreover, this formal pattern of repetition is matched by Jane's own recalling of the incident at moments of critical intensity throughout the novel: the recollection of the "frightful episode... in the dark and haunted chamber" following Jane's humiliating punishment by Brocklehurst at Lowood, for example, is a personal and narrative memory at once.

These structural repetitions cut across the "rules" of the Victorian novel's standard structure. *Jane Eyre* "seems to follow the developmental pattern of the *Bildungsroman*, whilst actually offering the very reverse of a progressive, linear history", says Sally Shutteworth. "Jane, as child, presents the same psychological formation as Jane in adulthood. The history she offers is that of a series of moments of conflict... the endless reiteration of the same." On this reading, not only the heroine, but the novelistic form which shapes her, are challenging conventional norms.

What does Jane learn at Lowood?

"Is she going by herself? ... What a long way!"... The coach drew up... I was taken from Bessie's neck, to which I clung with kisses.

> *"Be sure and take good care of her," cried she to the guard...*
>
> *The door was clapped to... and on we drove. Thus was I severed from Bessie and Gateshead: thus whirled away to unknown, and, as I then deemed, remote and mysterious regions. (5)*

The lonely distance of "preternatural length" which Jane travels from Gateshead to Lowood School is Jane's first journey in every sense. Begun in literal darkness and heading, in Jane's young mind, to an impenetrable and quasi-infernal destination, the journey has the unstoppable momentum of another kind of nightmare birth. From the point of the wrenching separation from Bessie, the one figure of maternity in Jane's orphaned childhood, through the strange sense of immensity and mortal apprehension Jane suffers en route, the journey resembles a terrifying descent into a new and strange existence – the fallen world itself.

> *I began to feel that we were getting very far indeed from Gateshead: we ceased to pass through towns; the country changed; great grey hills heaved up round the horizon: as twilight deepened, we descended a valley, dark with wood, and long after night had overclouded the prospect, I heard a wild wind rushing amongst trees. (5)*

The contours of this movement, like the shaping out of physical space in the red room, help transmit where Jane "lives", psychologically and emotionally, at these critical moments of growth.

At Lowood, Jane has almost literally to realise who or what she is in the world. When she first meets Helen Burns she is trying to understand the meaning of the words inscribed over the doors of the school .

> *"Lowood Institution... 'Let your light so shine before men that they may see your good works, and glorify your Father which is in heaven' St Matt v. 16... I read these words over and over again... endeavouring to make out a connection between the first words and the verse of scripture ...*
>
> *"Can you tell me what the writing on that stone over the door means? What is Lowood Institution?"*
>
> *"...A charity-school: you and I, and all the rest of us are charity-children. I suppose you are an orphan: are not either your father or your mother dead?... All the girls here have lost either one or both parents, and this is called an institution for educating orphans." (5)*

It is as though Jane were asking an infantile version of King Lear's impassioned question: "Who is it that can tell me who I am?" And at this raw stage of inchoate identity, she has to learn that the "connection" between Lowood and its proclaimed New Testament mission is as upside down and inverted as anything in the bitter social criticism of Dickens's novels. When Helen Burns impresses Jane as a model pupil who "retained the substance of the whole lesson and... was ready with answers on every point" (6), Jane is "expecting" Miss Scatcherd to "praise her attention"; instead, Helen is brutally admonished for a circumstance she could not have helped: "You dirty, disagreeable girl! You have never cleaned your nails this morning!" (6). In this abusively corrective environment, it is as if the meanings and value of reward and punishment, praise and blame, have become transposed.

Nowhere is this re-ordering more demonstrable than in Mr Brocklehurst's religious justifications for his school's regime:

"Humility is a Christian grace, and one peculiarly appropriate to the pupils of Lowood; I, therefore, direct that especial care shall be bestowed on its cultivation among them. I have studied how best to mortify in them the worldly sentiment of pride..." (4)

"My plan in bringing up these girls is... to render them hardy, patient and self-denying... put bread and cheese, instead of burnt porridge into these children's mouths, you may indeed feed their vile

*bodies, but you little think how you starve their
immortal souls!" (7)*

Humility and patience are *not* Christian virtues
here: on the contrary, they are utilitarian habits in
which the girls are trained in order to fit them for
their lowly social and monetary status. The most
terrifying aspect of Mr Brocklehurst, like
Dickens's Gradgrind in *Hard Times* before him, is
that he is presented as the narrow embodiment of
a principle – a straight "black pillar" is how he first
impresses Jane (4) – rather than as an example of
grimly exaggerated villainy.

The villains of Jane's childhood are
disconcertingly stupid and banal. And the
wholesale reversal of moral priorities which
Lowood represents is the more startling because it
emerges not from Dickensian comedic caricature,
but from one of the most celebrated sequences in
realist narrative in 19th-century fiction. "Harsh
physical discomfort [is] not merely piercingly
actual (the taste of the burnt porridge, the starved
arms wrapped in pinafores) but symbolic of a
loveless order of things," says Kathleen Tillotson.

Yet, as in Dickens, the intimation of a better
and morally straighter world, of which the
fictional world depicted is the corrupt distortion,
is present in often silenced or passive models of
goodness, whom Brontë has a quasi-Dickensian
facility for naming appropriately. The worshipped

headmistress, Miss Temple, and the religiously intense and literally feverish friend, Helen Burns, are Lowood's most potent instructors for Jane. After Helen's flogging at the hands of Miss Scatcherd, Jane expresses her outrage:

> "If I were in your place I should dislike her; I should resist her; if she struck me with that rod, I should get it from her hand; I should break it under her nose."
>
> "...If you did, Mr Brocklehurst would expel you from the school; that would be a great grief to your relations. It is far better to endure patiently a smart which nobody feels but yourself, than to commit a hasty action whose evil consequences will extend to all connected with you - and, besides, the Bible bids us return good for evil."...
>
> I heard her with wonder: I could not comprehend this doctrine of endurance: and still less could I understand or sympathise with the forbearance she expressed for her chastiser. (6)

"If I were in your place..." In fact, Helen is here occupying just the place in relation to Jane, which Jane took in relation to her own rebellious self, following her outburst to Mrs Reed, when she regretted the avenging impulse as unworthy of herself. Moreover, the older Helen offers to her young friend, in place of Old Testament vengeance, the alternative New Testament model of forgiveness – the "right" way as a corrective to Jane's "wrong" way. But Jane cannot learn this lesson when it might best serve her. Unjustly branded "a liar" and subjected to Brocklehurst's humiliating punishment ("mounted aloft... exposed to general view on a pedestal of infamy"), "an impulse of fury against Reed, Brocklehurst and Co., bounded in my pulses... I was no Helen Burns" (7). There is more than stubbornness and immaturity in Jane's resistance, however, just as there is a great deal more at stake in Helen's passivity than sentimental virtue:

> *"Life appears to me too short to be spent in nursing animosity, or registering wrongs. We are and must be, one and all, burdened with faults in this world: but the time will soon come when, I trust... sin will fall from us with this cumbrous frame of flesh, and only the spark of the spirit will remain... I live in calm, looking to the end."*
>
> *Helen's head, always drooping, sank a little lower as she finished this sentence. (6)*

"Helen had calmed me," says Jane after her disgrace. "But in the tranquillity she imparted there was an alloy of inexpressible sadness. I felt the impression of woe as she spoke." (8) Throughout these chapters, we feel that Helen's religious acceptance and equilibrium are not merely a means to tolerate the fact that she is dying: her faith and doctrine are only possible because she is dying. Yet just when Jane admits herself not to be Helen, it is Helen herself, in person and real, not impossibly ideal, who comes courageously forward as goodness embodied to find Jane's better self on her own behalf:

> *In passing, she lifted her eyes. What a strange light inspired them! What an extraordinary sensation that ray sent through me! How the new feeling bore me up... I mastered the rising hysteria, lifted up my head, and took a firm stand on the stool. (7)*

Even so, Helen's acquiescence in the face of dying cannot impart to Jane a complete philosophy for living. After eight years at a now-reformed Lowood, first as a pupil, then as a teacher, she finds the rebellious streak she embodies powerfully renewed: "School-rules, school-duties, school-habits... was what I knew of existence. And now I felt that it was not enough: I desired liberty; for liberty I gasped; for liberty I uttered a prayer" (10).

Significantly, this summons to fuller experience follows the departure of Miss Temple, the teacher-mentor who fills the maternal role in Jane's life in place of Bessie: Miss Temple's careful attentiveness to Jane when she first arrives at Lowood fulfils the wishes of Bessie's parting words. At the same time, the beginning of the Lowood stage of Jane's painful journey from child to adult formally invokes and anticipates its own closure. For when, in Chapter Ten, Jane is set to leave Lowood to take up the next stage of her life as governess at Thornfield, the maternal past she had resistantly left behind at Gateshead now comes back solicitously to take *its* leave.

> *"When I heard... that you were going to another part of the country, I thought I'd just set off and get a look at you before you were quite out of my reach... Well, who is it?" she asked in a voice and with a smile I half recognised; "you've not quite forgotten me, I think, Miss Jane?"*
>
> *In another second I was embracing and kissing her rapturously: "Bessie! Bessie! Bessie!" that was all I said. (10)*

These implicit markers of Jane's progress from child to adult are not merely literary flourishes, but an intrinsic part of the reader's experience of her story. For, while we inhabit Jane's suffering from inside her childish experience of it, we sense that her path belongs to a frame, a paradigm, a template for "growing up" everywhere, as well as for the despair of "growing into" the world of experience. The dark wood of her journey from Gateshead has Dante's example before her own. These echoes and connectedness to human-literary lineage and prior models help make her very wretchedness less vulnerable, more protected, and more bearable for us than it could possibly be for her.

What makes Rochester such a distinctive hero?

When Rochester arrives at Thornfield on a "tall steed" whose "rude noise" breaks the evening calm, accompanied by a "great dog" – "a lion-like creature with long hair and a huge head" (12) – he thunders into Jane's life as if destined to fulfil his role as powerful masculine incumbent of secluded, brooding Thornfield, with its "chill and vault-like air", "dark and spacious staircase", "long cold gallery" and "wide hall" hung with likenesses of "grim" personages and an oak-carved ebony clock. The "narrow, low, dim passage" of the third storey strikes Jane as resembling "a corridor in some Bluebeard's castle"; and here, while Jane's imagination prepares itself for a creature from fairy tale – "As this horse approached... I remembered certain of Bessie's tales wherein figured a North-of-England spirit" – the villain-hero himself seems about to appear through the dusk.

The most immediate literary antecedent of the Romantic Gothic aura which surrounds Rochester is the youthful writing of Charlotte Brontë herself. Her "legends of Angria", written in collaboration with her brother Branwell between 1834 and 1839, created an exotic fantasy world as the setting for a romantic saga of love, war, passion and revenge. Not only one of its principal characters, Duke Zamorna, but also its tales of scandal, betrayal and romantic domestic treachery provide a prototype for Rochester and his back story of sexual intrigue in Madeira and India.

Yet given the Brontë children's precociously extensive reading habits, the Angrian saga itself is inseparable from the influence of Gothic fiction and Romantic poetry, especially the work of Lord Byron, Charlotte's avowed literary hero. The exotic exploits and fiercely passionate individualism of Don Juan – hero of Byron's famous narrative poem of that name – is evoked in the successive association of Rochester with Persian King Ahasuerus, with the Grand Turk, and with a sultan in possession of a harem, as well as in his history of sexual licence. The hero's name itself, moreover, connotes the sensationally erotic verse of the Restoration poet, the 2nd Earl of Rochester.

But Rochester is also Brontë's version of Byron's Cain – from the biblical story in which Cain slays his brother Abel, and which Brontë described as a "magnificent poem". Like Milton's Satan before him – to which "fallen angel" and "snake-like tempter", Rochester significantly compares himself more than once – Cain is condemned to roam the earth, an isolated and resentful outcast, burdened with a curse of his own sinful making. The frequent association of Rochester with a "volcanic" secret nature – "that opened... now and then, in his eye, and closed again before one could fathom the strange depth" (18) – suggests forbidden, subterranean demonic powers.

But Brontë did not simply import these Romantic literary forebears into 19th-century "realist" fiction (though that is one aspect of her innovative genius); she also transformed and corrected them. "The man, the human being, broke the spell at once," says Jane, when horse and rider actually appear. The first thing "the man" does, moreover, is fall, which, if it is an implicit side glance to the fallenness of his past life and current spiritual state, also renders Rochester absolutely "the human being", a fallen fellow creature, vulnerably in need of another's succour, aid and care: "he laid a heavy hand on my shoulder, and leaning on me with some stress, limped to his horse" (12).

The powerful masculine presence of the novel is rendered as conspicuously powerless on first appearance as the titular heroine is remarkable for her plainness and indocility. Yet the character of Rochester, like that of Jane, does not simply

Michael Fassbender as Rochester in Cary Fukinaga's 2011 film

reverse the terms of its Romantic prototype; rather, the novel complicates and interrogates its model. For Rochester is always more, and often (comically) less, than the heroic category can normally contain. Where we expect highly charged feverish drama – at the sexually symbolic burning of his bedchamber, for example – we get the grimly realistic black humour of his cursing at the wetness of his bedclothes. Where Jane projects upon him the suavity of the successful suitor to Blanche Ingram, he confronts her emotionally in the humiliating pantomime gear of an old fortune-telling crone.

Alternatively, where we expect remorse and self-flagellation after the exposure of his precontracted marriage to Bertha, Rochester's strategies of seduction and narrowly aborted rape seem to emulate the worst excesses of Gothic male oppression. Yet what absolutely distinguishes Rochester as a Romantic hero is the fact that his deeply sexual nature is always treated as worthy of sympathetic seriousness and is involuntarily recognised by Jane as an expression of a passionate ferocity whose character is also deeply, and not merely residually, moral. Rochester is a fallen creature who, even as he baulks at his punishment, absolutely wants to be saved.

No other 19th-century hero (including Heathcliff) possesses this rich mix of emotional need and moral urgency, or the same intellectual awareness of his own spiritual predicament from within the animalism of the very body which has produced the ruin of his life. Only George Meredith's sequence poem *Modern Love* comes close to covering explicitly the same troubled human-sexual ground.

Yet Rochester does resemble Heathcliff insofar as both characters represent a sort of psycho-metaphysical experiment at the boundaries of generic fictional types. Robert B. Heilman was the first to point out that

if in Rochester we see only an Angrian-Byronic hero... we miss what is most significant, the exploration [and] opening up of new areas of feeling in intersexual relationships... That discovery of passion, that rehabilitation of the extra-rational, which is the historical office of Gothic, is no longer oriented in marvellous circumstance but moves deeply into the lesser known realities of human life.

Rochester finds his real legacy, suggest both Heilman and John Maynard, in the great questions of sexuality and identity posed by D.H. Lawrence's *Lady Chatterley's Lover*, which met with the same outrage as *Jane Eyre* on first publication.

What is the significance of Jane's role as governess?

The crimson curtain hung before the arch: slight as the separation this drapery formed from the party in the adjoining salon, they spoke in so low a key that nothing of their conversation could be distinguished...

"Why, I suppose you have a governess for [Adèle]: I saw a person with her just now – is she gone? Oh, no! there she still is behind the window-curtain. You pay her of course." (17)

Jane's situation during the house party at Thornfield, where the winning socialite and aspirant wife of Rochester, Blanche Ingram, takes centre stage, not only repeats Jane's past marginalisation at Gateshead (where we first see her in the "double retirement" of a window-seat, the "the red moreen curtain drawn nearly close" (1)). It also literalises her social position in the present household. A chief prerequisite of the governess was that she should possess all the respectability of ladyhood without ever enjoying its status. She must be demonstrably at home in genteel company, without ever being truly accepted into it. She must model all conventional feminine accomplishments, such as music, drawing, French, taste in dress – in short, everything that made a woman marriageable – without ever looking to be fulfilled in that state herself.

An "ambiguous" and "difficult" relation to the host family, with expectation of "neither companionship nor sympathy", were "discomforts inseparable from [the governess's] position", wrote Anna Brownell Jameson in 1846 ("The Relative Social Position of Mothers and Governesses"). The image of pained loneliness and degrading deprivation which accompanies the abiding image of the Victorian governess finds its blueprint and chief source equally in *Jane Eyre* and in Charlotte Brontë's own life. In a letter to

Elizabeth Gaskell, Brontë wrote :

> If teaching only were requisite, it would be smooth and easy; but it is the living in other people's houses – the estrangement from one's real character – the adoption of a cold, frigid, apathetic exterior, that is painful.

But *Jane Eyre* exploits the ambiguity of the governess's position in complex and powerful ways. Burdened with the precarious independence of seeking her own living, Jane is able to ape the traditional trajectory of the male hero (where moral, social and financial "careers" are intertwined, as in *David Copperfield* or *Nicholas Nickleby*), in a way impossible to a socially more comfortable heroine who was often, by that very token, more constricted. ("While I live," says the uncle of Caroline Helstone, heroine of Charlotte Brontë's later novel, *Shirley*, "you shall not turn out as a governess. I will not have it said that my niece is a governess.") The very disadvantages of Jane's situation means that she embodies a unique perspective on the expectations and limitations of conventional femininity which can find legitimate and "safe" expression as part of the "plight" of the governess:

> *I longed for a power of vision... which might reach the busy world, towns, regions full of life I had*

heard of but never seen... I desired more of practical experience than I possessed; more of intercourse with my kind, of acquaintance with variety of character, than was here within my reach. (12)

As Kathryn Hughes says, Jane the governess is at once a daring alter ego and a surrogate and

THE GOVERNESS

The governess became a familiar figure in 19th-century fiction, with some 140 novels featuring a governess published between 1814 and 1865. One of the very few employment options for penniless and unprovided-for women, the situation of the governess was often oppressive. Yet, as Kathryn Hughes and Mary

Poovey point out, the attention the governess's distress received was disproportionate to the extent of the problem and indicates cultural anxieties which centre in "the tension which the governess embodies – concerning social respectability, sexual morality and financial self-reliance".

The governess is culturally significant, says Poovey, "because of the proximity she bears to two of the most important Victorian representations of woman – the figure who epitomised the domestic ideal, and the figure who threatened to destroy it" – by being "independent" professionally (earning her own income) as well as sexually (by definition single and marriageable, degradedly vulnerable, and living at close spokeswoman for all middle-class women. As a lady exempt from some of the more constricting aspects of ladyhood, the governess could be depicted in an unusual and uncomfortable situation while, at another level, allowing Brontë to examine genteel femininity in action.

Moreover, Jane's very subordination confers a privileged vision, which – while to all appearances

---

quarters with husbands and sons).

Significantly, given the doubling of Jane and Bertha in the novel, anxieties about the governess's sexual neutrality linked her in the Victorian mind to two figures of sexual depravity – the fallen woman and the lunatic. The novel with which *Jane Eyre* invites most immediate comparison is *Vanity Fair*, published earlier the same year, and to whose author, William Thackeray, Charlotte Brontë dedicated her own novel. These novels together marked "the governess's arrival at the heart of the English novel", says Hughes.

The aptly named Becky Sharp, protagonist of *Vanity Fair*, rises through the social ranks from governess to lady by every disreputable means at her disposal – theft, fraud, deceit – offending all Victorian mores of honesty and decency, while ironically exposing in the process a good many of those belonging to "respectable" society itself. *Jane Eyre* reversed the genre almost as it began, by substituting an authentically passionate first-person protagonist – plain, oppressed and mistreated – for *Vanity Fair*'s anti-heroine and her cynically attractive sexual exploitation; an engaged, first-person voice for Thackeray's detached, ironic third-person narration; and a penetrating analysis of the female psyche for an anatomy of social manners and misdemeanours.

While Blanche Ingram would not be out of place in the society of *Vanity Fair*, in conscientiously adjusted to her situation ("I dressed myself with care, solicitous to be neat... and put on my black frock, Quaker-like as it was..." (11)) – she consciously exercises. She is a watcher, who sees Rochester's faults, her pupil Adèle's spoilt inanity, and Blanche Ingram's deadness and poverty of life. This possibility of being everywhere and nowhere – an insider-outsider –

Jane Eyre herself "the love story, the woman question and the governess (social) problem coalesce", as Inga-Stina Ewbank has put it. For Terry Eagleton, however, the distance between Becky Sharp and Jane Eyre is more apparent than actual. Brontë's protagonists, says Eagleton, represent

an extraordinarily contradictory amalgam of smouldering rebelliousness and prim conventionalism, gushing Romantic fantasy and canny hard-headedness, quivering sensitivity and blunt rationality. It is, in fact, a contradiction closely related to their roles as governesses... The governess is a servant, trapped within a rigid social function which demands industriousness,

subservience and self-sacrifice: but she is also an 'upper' servant... furnished with an imaginative awareness and cultivated sensibility... She lives at that ambiguous point in the social structure at which two worlds – an internal one of emotional hungering, and an external one of harsh mechanical necessity – meet and collide.

For Eagleton, Jane's mode of employment and orphan status "leaves the self a free, blank, 'pre-social' atom: free to be injured and exploited but free also to progress, move through the class structure". The "deep bourgeois ethic" of the novel is shown in its strategy of turning submissive conventionalism into a means of self-advancement •

is itself a kind of protean release from the stereotyped role of spinster governess. It is analogous, as well, to the habits of the novelist (also, like Charlotte Brontë, a woman of uncertain means and, in Victorian society, of ambivalent standing). Indeed, it is part of the power of the novel that the craft of character and author are often closely identified. At the house party, for example, Jane first overhears the conversation relating to herself as governess, as the disregarded and neglected audience of a social drama in which she is the victimised inferior. The tables are then defiantly turned when Jane's superior insight exposes the poverty of their minds with all the authority of an omniscient narrator's definitive word.

> *She [Blanche Ingram] was very showy, but she was not genuine: she had a fine person, many brilliant attainments; but her mind was poor, her heart barren by nature: nothing bloomed spontaneously on that soil; no unforced natural fruit delighted by its freshness. (18)*

At such moments, this often vulnerable first-person narration becomes the vehicle of an accomplished revenge in which the ends of author and character seem inseparable.

But nowhere is the potency of Jane's paradoxical freedom from rigidity of place and role more pronounced than in her relations with Rochester. In Jane's first "official" private meeting with Rochester as his employee, he imperiously exercises his right (not uncommon for the master of the household) to summon the governess for company and conversation more agreeable to his intellect and tastes than either his ward, Adèle, or housekeeper, Mrs Fairfax, can offer. Yet the ambiguities, which make possible such otherwise anomalous and quasi-adulterous relations between non-married men and women in bourgeois households, seem mutually exploited.

> *"It would please me now to draw you out – to learn more of you – therefore speak – ."*
>
> *Instead of speaking, I smiled: and not a very complacent or submissive smile either.*
>
> *"Speak," he urged.*
>
> *"What about, sir?"*
>
> *"Whatever you like. I leave both the choice of subject and the manner of treating it entirely to yourself."*
>
> *Accordingly, I sat and said nothing: "If he expects me to talk for the mere sake of talking and showing off, he will find he has addressed himself to the wrong person," I thought…*
>
> *"Stubborn?" he said, "and annoyed. Ah, it is consistent. I put my request in an absurd, almost insolent form. Miss Eyre, I beg your pardon. The fact is, once for all, I don't wish to treat you like an*

Orson Welles with Margaret O'Brien and
Joan Fontaine in a scene from the 1943 film

inferior: that is (correcting himself), I claim only
such superiority as must result from twenty years'
difference in age and a century's advance in
experience." (14)

As Rochester's demand is at once an exercise of
control ("Speak") and, paradoxically, a liberal
relaxation of his power ("Whatever you like"), so
Jane's silence is both proper resistance to the
former *and* "stubborn" refusal of the latter, as if to
insist upon a more voluntary liberty: "This is how I

do what I like."

But this isn't simply the old rebellious Jane. Rather, what the master-servant roles allow here is something close to the kind of reversal that takes place between Shakespearean heroes and heroines and the licensed fool who, partly by virtue of subordination and the permission of his master or mistress, knows the characters better than they know themselves. Certainly Jane's wit is equal to this role.

JANE THE ARTIST

The paintings which Jane reveals to Rochester early in her time at Thornfield (13) show the influence of her childhood fascination with Bewick (the pictures depict, successively, a cormorant, an iceberg and the evening star); and the visionary landscapes – wild, dramatic, uncertain of meaning – are continuous with the dream life Jane experiences throughout the novel. What Rochester sympathetically examines in these paintings, then, is an expression of Jane's inner life. Painting has been by turns her safety valve in loneliness and her confidant: at Lowood she "feasted... on the spectacle of ideal drawings, which I saw in the dark; all the work of my own hands: freely pencilled houses and trees, picturesque rocks and ruins" (10), and her actual portfolio was produced, Jane tells Rochester, "in the

"I don't think, sir, you have a right to command me, merely because you are older than I, or because you have seen more of the world than I have – your claim to superiority depends on the use you have made of your time and experience." (14)

When, at the house party, Rochester disguises himself as the gypsy fortune teller – in an incident of cross-dressing which places the master now in the subordinate and socially ostracised role usually occupied by Jane the servant – Brontë's dialogue relishes the potential for witty power-

last two vacations I spent at Lowood, when I had no other occupation".

Jane's art is a specifically Romantic form of expressionism and brings with it Romantic creative anxieties about the gap between conception and execution, and the difficulty of giving form to what is essentially and elusively inexpressible. "'I was tormented by the contrast between my idea and my handiwork ... I had imagined something which I was quite powerless to realise.' 'Not quite [says Rochester]: you have secured the shadow of your thought.'"

These considerations connect not only to Brontë's own gifts as an artist, but, reflexively, to her primary métier as writer. In the pivotal passage (12) where Jane laments her specifically female form of "restlessness" on the third storey at Thornfield, her "sole relief" from the pain of agitation is to "allow my mind's eye to dwell on whatever bright visions rose before it... best of all, to open my inward ear to a tale that was never ended – a tale my imagination created, and narrated continuously; quickened with all of incident, life, fire, feeling, that I desired play and sexual negotiation which this further temporary release from "official" rules of social discourse allows:

> *"I have... a quick eye, and a quick brain."*
> *"You need them all in your trade."*
> *"I do; especially when I have customers like you to deal with. Why don't you tremble?"*
> *"I'm not cold."*
> *"Why don't you turn pale?"*
> *"I am not sick.*

and had not in my actual existence".

The potential for the imagination to compensate for the privations of female experience in the 19th century is not to be underestimated. For Sandra Gilbert and Susan Gubar, indeed, fear of the power of the female creative imagination by female writers themselves, who were trespassing on a predominantly male literary domain, helped produce the "monsters" in their novels (Bertha, Frankenstein's monster) as displaced symptoms of authorial anxiety.

What *Jane Eyre* offers, however, is not an alternative existence, but a truer *form* for Jane's/Charlotte's "actual" one. Finding no preconceived or conventional social or literary model available which answered to the meaning of her life, Jane Eyre represents Charlotte Brontë's Romantic-artistic and ontological struggle to allow her life authentically to speak and shape itself in the form and language of the novel. The very amorphousness of the book – with its mix of genres, voices, and, like Jane's paintings, its exploration of new dimensions and realities – is testimony to that creative effort •

"Why don't you consult my art?"
"I'm not silly." (18)

"The repartee of the lovers is one of the joys of the novel and the cross-threats a form of sexual courting," observes John Maynard. But this sharpness is the reverse of the exploitative playfulness of *Vanity Fair*, precisely because we are always aware that Rochester speaks to Jane from the far side of experience: "a trite commonplace sinner, hackneyed in all the poor, petty dissipations with which the rich and worthless try to put on life" (14). If Rochester places Jane in the role of involuntary confidant – "it is not your forte to talk of yourself, but to listen" (14) – it is because he finds in Jane something he needs: a confessor. "You, with your gravity, considerateness, and caution were made to be the recipient of secrets" (15). Rochester's fallen vulnerability, nesting inside his masterly position and manner, makes the power relations between the pair particularly subtle, allowing, paradoxically, a greater equality than the standard romantic relationship (with Blanche Ingram, for example) can achieve. "I find it impossible to be conventional with you," says Rochester (14); and Jane's sense of sharing an authentic intimacy and discourse with him is reciprocal: "The ease of his manner freed me from painful restraint... I felt at times, as if he were my relation, rather than my

TEN FACTS
ABOUT *JANE EYRE*

1.

Jane Eyre was Charlotte Brontë's second novel.
Her first, *The Professor*, was initially presented (in
a letter to publishers) as part of "a work of fiction,
consisting of three distinct and unconnected
tales..." The other "tales" were Emily Brontë's
Wuthering Heights and Anne's *Agnes Grey*. While
Charlotte's sisters found publishers, *The Professor*
was rejected seven times, the final refusal showing
admiration for the author's "literary promise" and
inviting a three-volume novel, with more "startling
incident" and "thrilling excitement". This became
Jane Eyre.

2.

Jane Eyre was first published in 1847 under the
pseudonym Currer Bell. *Wuthering Heights* and
Agnes Grey appeared in the same year, under the
names Ellis and Acton Bell. The "ambiguous"

names were chosen, wrote Charlotte in a Biographical Notice for the 1850 edition of *Wuthering Heights*, because the sisters were wary of "assuming Christian names positively masculine" yet "did not like to declare ourselves women" for fear that their work would not be impartially judged.

3.
While some early reviewers couldn't believe the novel was written by a female hand, others were not so deceived. "The writer is evidently a woman," wrote George Henry Lewes, and Elizabeth Barrett Browning was "astounded when sensible people said otherwise". "It is a woman's writing, but whose," wondered Thackeray, to whom, on receiving his "respect and thanks", Brontë dedicated the second edition of *Jane Eyre*. ("One good word from such a man is worth pages of praise from ordinary judges," she wrote.)

4.
In October 2009 a Mills & Boon poll found Mr Rochester to be "the most romantic character in literature". Rochester received more votes than both *Pride and Prejudice*'s Mr Darcy and *Far From the Madding Crowd*'s Gabriel Oak.

5.
Charlotte thought of literary fame as "a passport to the society of clever people", according to a school friend, but when at last she achieved it "she

lamented that it was of no use" – her sisters and brothers were dead and her sufferings had left her unable to bear society. Between the publication of *Jane Eyre* in 1847 and *Shirley* in 1849, Branwell, Emily and Anne all died. "I felt that the house was all silent – the rooms were all empty. I remembered where the three were laid – in what narrow dark dwellings – never more to reappear on earth. So the sense of desolation and bitterness took possession of me." (Elizabeth Gaskell's *The Life of Charlotte Brontë*).

6.
Two famous 19-century works were influenced by *Jane Eyre*. In an apparently unconscious borrowing from the Brontë work she deeply admired, Elizabeth Barrett Browning's novel-poem *Aurora Leigh* (1857) concludes with the hero, Romney Leigh, being blinded as a result of a fire, before being reunited with the heroine. In Henry James's *The Turn of the Screw* (1898), the neurotic governess, obsessed with her employer, asks herself: "Was there a secret at Bly? an insane, an unmentionable relative kept in unsuspected confinement?"

7.
Within a year of its publication, *Jane Eyre* had been dramatised for the stage, and more than 10 other adaptations soon followed. The Gothic elements of the novel lent themselves to the chief 19th-century genre for popular entertainment – melodrama. Jane's rebelliousness was toned down

and she was generally characterised as fragile, despondent and defeated.

8.
The most famous novel inspired by *Jane Eyre* is Daphne du Maurier's *Rebecca* (1938) in which an erstwhile lady's companion marries into the gentry, only to find her new home, Manderley, haunted by Rebecca, her husband's first wife.

9.
Wide Sargasso Sea (1966) offers a prequel to *Jane Eyre*. Bertha Mason, the Caribbean heiress and first Mrs Rochester, is rechristened Antoinette (her middle name in *Jane Eyre*) and is allowed to tell her own story in extended monologue. She is depicted as a victim because of her Creole status, accepted neither by black or white cultures in a post-slavery world. Submissive and exploited, she surrenders to Rochester's sexual demands and is afterwards rejected for "intemperance" and is betrayed by her husband's promiscuous infidelity.

10.
There were no fewer than 12 silent film versions of *Jane Eyre* and one "talkie" before the acclaimed 1943 film, co-written by Aldous Huxley and starring Joan Fontaine and Orson Welles. There have been many modern film and TV versions, among them Franco Zeffirrelli's 1996 casting of Charlotte Gainsbourg as a pale, plain yet independent-spirited Jane opposite supermodel Elle Macpherson's Blanche Ingram.

master" (15).

Significantly, it is when Jane has become betrothed to him, and he confers upon her the officially sanctioned status of wife – "soon to be Jane Rochester" – and seeks to deck her in the dress and jewels befitting her elevated station, that she almost immediately senses a loss of their privileged sense of equality: she feels "an ape in a harlequin's jacket, a jay in borrowed plumes", declares "I will not be your English Céline Varens", and refuses to give up the independence of her "governessing slavery" until the marriage (24). It is one of the most strident attacks on marriage as institutionalised "slavery" in any fiction of the period.

What is at stake in the master-servant ambiguity becomes clear when Jane puts out the fire in Rochester's bedchamber:

> *"Why, you have saved my life! – snatched me from a horrible and excruciating death! and you walk past me as if we were mutual strangers! At least shake hands."*
>
> *He held out his hand; I gave him mine: he took it first in one, then in both his own.*
>
> *"You have saved my life: I have a pleasure in owing you so immense a debt. I cannot say more. Nothing else that has being would have been tolerable to me in the character of creditor for such an obligation: but you; it is different;– I feel your*

benefits no burden, Jane."

He paused; gazed at me: words almost visible trembled on his lips, – but his voice was checked.

"Good night again, sir. There is no debt, benefit, burden, obligation, in the case." (15)

Jane has been his servant in the most extreme sense, offering the deepest service, saving his life. When he proffers equality, she, in asking for nothing in return, gives him it back. It is a moment which carries a central message of the novel, one which both protagonists have yet to learn fully: that love has nothing to do with servitude in the narrow sense, but is inconceivable without some higher ideal of service.

Why is Bertha so important?

In the deep shade... a figure ran backwards and forwards... Whether beast or human being... it snatched and growled... gazed wildly at her visitors... [At] Mr Rochester... the lunatic sprang and grappled his throat viciously, and laid her teeth to his cheek: they struggled. She was a big woman, in stature almost equalling her husband, and corpulent besides: she showed virile force in

the contest – more than once she almost throttled
him, athletic as she was... Mr Rochester then
turned to the spectators: he looked at them with a
smile both acrid and desolate.

"That is my wife," *said he. "Such is the sole*
conjugal embrace I am ever to know – such are the
endearments which are to solace my leisure hours!
And this *is what I wished to have (laying his hand*
on my shoulder): this young girl, who stands so
grave and quiet at the mouth of hell... Compare
these clear eyes with the red balls yonder – this
face with that mask – this form with that bulk."
(26)

In her influential early feminist reading of *Jane Eyre*, Adrienne Rich finds in Rochester's insistence upon the absolute distinction between Bertha's sexually aggressive animalism and Jane's puritanically bridal virginity a crystallisation of the sexual double standards of Victorian masculinity: "the nineteenth-century loose woman might have sexual feelings, but the nineteenth-century *wife* did not and must not". What is imprisoned in the third-storey attic at Thornfield, on this reading, is a sexual virility and excess – an appetite of "giant propensities... the most gross, impure, depraved I ever saw" – which threatens to encroach (and, with literal repetition, does so in this novel) on the protected spaces of domesticated femininity. Is Bertha a warning against the perils of passionate sexual inclination, or a critique of Victorian repression of female sexuality and the associated distortions of that repression, or both? With all the potency of monsters elsewhere in female Gothic fiction – Mary Shelley's *Frankenstein*, above all, perhaps – the meaning of Bertha is unsettlingly protean and multiple.

At one level, Bertha focalises Victorian cultural anxieties, in ways not dissimilar, significantly, to the figures of governess and child with whom Jane is aligned. The two figures in Victorian psychological discourse "who demarcated the sphere of excess", says Sally Shuttleworth, were "the passionate child and the madwoman". At another level, her dramatic power within the novel is really that of giving disturbing physical presence to Jane's psychological fears. When, under his disguise as a fortune teller, Rochester intimately ventriloquises Jane's habitual suppression of her stronger feelings, he also thereby locates and draws out those feelings – finding the Bertha inside Jane, as it were:

> *Reason sits firm and holds the reins, and she will not let the feelings burst away and hurry her to wild chasms. The passions may rage furiously... and the desires may imagine... but judgment shall still have the last word... Strong wind, earthquake-shock and fire may pass by: but I shall follow the*

guiding of that still small voice which interprets
the dictates of conscience. (19)

All the feared inverse possibilities of Jane's measured demeanour – energies unleashed and uncontrolled in primal snarls, growls, demoniac laughter – are embodied within Bertha as Jane's alter ego. That is why there is a successive narrative overlap or proximity between the incidents of Bertha's escape from captivity into inhabited areas of the house and moments of high emotional intensity for Jane. The burning of Rochester's bedchamber (where the simple narrative facts – *Jane* wakes to put out *Bertha's* fire in *Rochester's* bed – are also a Freudian tale of the subconscious) is the immediate sequel to Rochester's recounting to Jane of the erotic back story of his guardianship of Adèle (who is the product, apparently, of Rochester's passionate affair with French opera dancer Céline Varens).

More shocking than the revelation, perhaps, is Jane's absence of shock and daring request to know the whole: "I ventured to recall him to the point," says Jane, when Rochester's narrative digresses (15). The confession leads to Jane's admission that she is "so happy, so gratified... with this new interest added to life"; "my thin crescent destiny seemed to enlarge, the blanks of existence were filled up". She cannot sleep, she tells her

Biting by Paula Rego, who made a series of lithographs based on the story of Jane Eyre

confidential reader, on the night of the fire, "for thinking of his look". The conflagration which immediately follows – "Tongues of flame darted round the bed... In the midst of blaze and vapour, Mr Rochester lay stretched motionless..." – is an externalised representation of the incipient passion tamely contained within Jane's conscious admissions: his face was "the object I best liked to see" and "his presence in a room more cheering than the brightest fire". However much Jane controls her own first-person narrative, and the reader's response to herself and her history, she cannot control – so Bertha's incontrovertible presence suggests – her own deeper and truer self and story.

For Bertha is not just what Jane could or might be. She represents what Jane demonstrably is, at some level. When Rochester dramatically points to the antipathetic opposition between Jane and Bertha – "Compare" – he is in fact making explicit the connection between them, a connection which is submerged during most of the Thornfield section of the novel. When Jane finds her "sole relief" on the third storey of Thornfield, venting the "restlessness" which "agitated me to pain sometimes", she not only hears the "eccentric murmurs" of the other occupant of that part of the house but replicates the prisoner's "rebellious" desire for liberty and even apes her very actions, walking "backwards and forwards" along the corridor (12). Moreover, the attic which imprisons Bertha is directly analogous to the red room to which Jane was banished as a child, precisely as punishment for her own deeds of excess (a "bad animal", "frantic", "beside myself; or rather out of myself" (2)), and where she experienced the "warm... mood of the revolted slave" with its "bitter vigour" (2).

Rochester himself has contributed to this trail of associative likeness in calling Jane "bewitched" (13), "a witch, a sorceress" (15). Thus it is a moment of great psychological significance, directly recalling the red room incident, when, on the eve of her wedding, and "for the second time in my life – only the second time", Jane becomes "insensible from terror" at what she sees in the mirror:

> *"It seemed, sir, a woman, tall and large, with thick and dark hair hanging long down her back... [dress] white and straight... She took my veil from its place; she held it up, gazed at it long, and then she threw it over her own head... At that moment I saw the reflection of the visage and features quite distinctly in the dark oblong glass... Fearful and ghastly to me... I never saw a face like it... it was a savage face... The fiery eye glared upon me– she thrust up her candle close to my face... her lurid visage flamed over mine and I lost consciousness." (10)*

While at the level of plot and public story, Bertha is Jane's rival – the other Mrs Rochester – at the level of inner story Bertha is Jane's dark double, the ferocious secret self she has been trying to suppress since Gateshead. In this respect, Bertha is the extreme version of models and counter-models of female being which operate throughout the book – from Mrs Reed and her daughters, through Helen Burns and Miss Temple, to Blanche Ingram and later the Rivers sisters. Ultimately, says Adrienne Rich, "Jane's instinct for self-preservation... must save her from becoming this woman by curbing her imagination at the limits of what is bearable for a powerless woman in the England of the 1840s".

But Bertha's meaning does not end with Jane. If her existence divides Jane and Rochester, her psychological resonance – as a thing inadmissible or denied and for that reason more damagingly powerful – is also what unites them. If anything, what Bertha means in relation to Rochester is more disturbing than the rich, fluid symbolism which attaches her to Jane, precisely because she so singularly and literally reflects his nature.

"I have a past existence, a series of deeds, a colour of life to contemplate within my own breast... I might have been as good as you – wiser – almost as stainless. I envy you your peace of mind, your

*clean conscience, your unpolluted memory. Little
girl, a memory without blot or contamination must
be an exquisite treasure – an inexhaustible source
of pure refreshment." (14)*

Bertha also stands in this novel for the visible
burden of polluted memory, past mistakes,
contaminated conscience – for sin incarnate and
refusing to die. You can change, urges Jane,
resolutely; no, I cannot, says Rochester, in equally
earnest belief that he is damned. In this respect,
Bertha's meaning is as much religious and moral
as it is psychological and sexual, and part of the
astonishing power of this book is that these
aspects of human experience are never credibly
separable.

THE POLITICS OF MADNESS

In the past three decades, it has become critical orthodoxy to regard Bertha's representation of madness, sexuality and savagery as resonant of Victorian discourses for demarcating the "Other", especially gendered and racially inflected notions of excessive or uncontrolled sexuality, and of insanity or irrational states of consciousness. The figure of savage Bertha also draws on Victorian constructions of colonial identity in a novel in which the uncle of the heroine is connected to the Mason family through colonial commerce, while Bertha's outbreaks of violence connote slave riots in the English colonies as well as political rebellions at home.

The first influential and now orthodox political-critical reading of madness in *Jane Eyre* came from Sandra Gilbert and Susan Gubar:

Jane's confrontation with Rochester's mad wife Bertha, is the book's central confrontation... not with her own sexuality but with her own imprisoned "hunger, rebellion and rage". On a figurative and psychological level... Bertha is... Jane's truest, darkest double: she is the angry aspect of the orphan child, the ferocious secret self Jane has been trying to repress ever since her days at Gateshead.

Psychological "doubles" are a staple of 19th-century Gothic fiction: Mary Shelley's *Frankenstein*, Bram Stoker's *Dracula* and Robert Louis Stevenson's *Strange Case of Jekyll and Hyde* posit twinned characters or selves, which roughly correspond to Freud's notions of ego and id,* the one representing the socially conformist or conventional personality, the other externalising the free, uninhibited, often criminal self. In *Jane Eyre*'s brand of female Gothic, the confined mad wife is expressive of every aspect of female experience – sexuality, desire for independence, frustration at limitation – which Victorian social mores deemed unfeminine and which legally and socially it sought to restrain and suppress. Gothic fantasy "characteristically attempts to compensate for lack resulting from

* Id, ego and super-ego are the three parts of our psyche, according to Sigmund Freud's model. The id refers, essentially, to our uncoordinated instincts, the super-ego plays a critical, moralising role, the ego is the reasoned, realistic part which mediates between the desires of the id and the restraint of the super-ego.

cultural constraints: it is a literature of desire, which seeks that which is experienced as absence and loss", says Rosemary Jackson in *The Literature of Subversion*.

In *Charlotte Brontë and Victorian Psychology*, however, Sally Shuttleworth argues that Gilbert and Gubar's reading is "resolutely ahistorical, failing... to place Brontë's work firmly within the context of Victorian psychological discourse", while suggesting that the issue of madness cannot be isolated from the wider social and economic context which actively defines it. Shuttleworth follows Michel Foucault's thesis in *Madness and Civilisation*, which argues that the 19th century witnessed the emergence of a new economy of individual and social life, centred on the regulation of the forces of the body and controlled through surveillance. With the rise of secular capitalism, a new interiorised notion of selfhood arose and, concomitantly, new techniques of power designed to penetrate the inner secrets of this hidden domain.

Psychiatry emerged as a science dedicated to decoding the external signs of the body in order to reveal the concealed inner play of forces which constitute individual subjectivity, while psychological and social discourses sought to define the elusive concept "normal", as opposed to "hysterical" or "mad". The new paradigm emerging in physiological and social discourse was one in which the old religious divide between health and sickness, good and ill, had been supplanted by a sliding scale of the normal and pathological, where insanity and health were not absolutes but states of health pushed to extremes.

> The incipient parallel... between Jane and the "mad" Bertha turns on the issue of the flow of energy: at what point does productive forcefulness turn into self-destructive anarchy? For a Victorian woman the question was particularly fraught since women were biologically defined as creatures of excess, throbbing with reproductive energy which had to be sluiced away each month, yet could not be dammed up or controlled without real threat to the balance of the psyche. In constructing the parallel histories of Jane and Bertha, Brontë constantly negotiates between these different models of womanhood, trying to find an image of female empowerment and control which would not also be a negation of femininity.

In this reading, Shuttleworth builds on and extends two earlier influential political readings of the novel. In *Myths of Power: A Marxist Study of the Brontës,* Terry Eagleton's thesis is that *Jane Eyre* "negotiates passionate self-fulfilment on terms which preserve the social and moral conventions intact, and so preserve intact the submissive, enduring, everyday self which adheres to them". The self thus achieves preservation and advancement in accord with the bourgeois ethic and class structure of Victorian industrial capitalism.

> To allow passionate imagination premature rein is to be exposed, vulnerable and ultimately self-defeating: it is to be locked in the red room, enticed into bigamous marriage, ensnared... in a hopelessly consuming love. Passion springs from the very core of the self and yet is hostile, alien, invasive; the world of internal fantasy must therefore be locked away, as the mad Mrs Rochester stays locked up on an upper floor of Thornfield. The inner world must yield of necessity to the practical virtues of caution, tact [which] satisfy restrictive convention and lead ultimately to a fulfilling transcendence of it.

While Jane's sexual passion is "strikingly imaged in the grotesque figure of Bertha", Bertha is "masculine, black-visaged and almost the same height as her husband" and thus "appears also as a repulsive symbol of Rochester's sexual drive". The novel, says Eagleton, seeks to "domesticate that drive" in order that "in the end the outcast bourgeoise achieves more than a humble place at the fireside: she also gains independence vis à vis the upper class and the right to engage in the process of taming it".

For Gayatri Spivak, the figure of Bertha Mason is likewise to be interpreted in the context of Victorian political ideology and discourse, but for Spivak, it is the ideology of imperialism – an ideology that went hand in hand with capitalist individualism – which provides the discursive field. In this reading, the racially ambiguous Bertha, neither white nor black, occupies the position of the forces to be oppressed and obliterated so as to ensure the emergence of a homogeneous central subject.

> Through Bertha Mason, the white Jamaican Creole, Brontë produces a human/animal colonial subject for the glorification of the social and civilising mission of the British imperial colonizer [variously figured in the novel as Jane the educator/teacher, Rochester the colonial adventurer, St John the civilising missionary]. The dark and untamed Other must set fire to the house and kill herself, be sacrificed as an insane animal, so that Jane Eyre can become the feminist individualist heroine of British fiction.

Where is sex in *Jane Eyre*? What is love?

To the first question the answer often seems simply: "sex is in Bertha" – albeit imperfectly contained – or "in Rochester", the two obviously sexual creatures of the book. If Bertha seems to offer a cautionary illustration of the dangers of excessive sexual appetite, Rochester's example is much more equivocal.

We learn early that Rochester, not yet in middle age, has given himself up to a life of degenerate pleasure in reactive despair at the prospect of a life "hampered, burdened, cursed" (14), as a consequence of the thrill-seeking indulgences of his younger self. However duped Rochester might have been by his own and Bertha's family into becoming "bound to a wife at once intemperate and unchaste" (27), his own sensual nature and responsiveness to sexually available women made him susceptible to this trickery – "I was dazzled, stimulated: my senses were excited" – just as, in relation to Céline Varens, it made him vulnerable to betrayal. In Rochester, however, sensuality is a form of excuse, offered in mitigation of past fault– an aspect of his youthfulness and "inexperience".

Moreover, his sensuality is as essential to his allure as it is to Bertha's monstrosity; the very

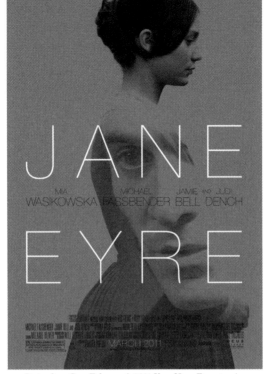

Poster from Cary Fukunaga's 2011 film of Jane Eyre *starring Mia Wasikowska (Jane) and Michael Fassbender (Rochester).*

burdens of his promiscuous past (guilt, resentment, Bertha herself) unravel only in intriguing retrospect, adding to his "ireful and thwarted", "grimly grimacing" demeanour, and the "morose, almost malignant scowl [which] blackened his features" (15). Neither "handsome" nor "heroic-looking" (12), he embodies a kind of baulked primitive energy. At the sight of Thornfield, he first recounts to Jane his compromising past:

*He ground his teeth and was silent: he arrested his
step and struck his boot against the hard ground.
Some hated thought seemed to have him in his
grip, and to hold him so tightly that he could not
advance... Pain, shame, ire, impatience, disgust,
detestation , seemed momentarily to hold a
quivering conflict in the large pupil dilating under
his ebon eyebrow. Wild was the wrestle which
should be paramount; but another feeling rose and
triumphed: something hard and cynical; self-
willed and resolute: it settled his passion and
petrified his countenance. (15)*

The more Rochester hides his secret self, the more
it seems to claim its own forms of alarming
physiological and outward expression – as if the
price of shutting Bertha in is the constant risk of
being turned violently inside-out by the sheer
force of his own vital energies. When Bertha's
existence is revealed and Jane announces her
intention to leave, his look is "that of a man who is
just about to burst an insufferable bond and
plunge headlong into wild license. I saw that in
another moment, and with one impetus of frenzy
more, I should be able to do nothing with him... A
movement of repulsion, flight, fear, would have
sealed my doom, – and his" (27). Rochester's wild
temperament, barely restrained and posing at this
moment a very real threat of sexual violence, is
among the book's most constant and frightening

versions of madness confined.

From the start of their relationship, as we have seen, Jane represents to Rochester a monitory corrective to his wild agony:

> *"Since happiness is irrevocably denied me, I have a right to get pleasure out of life: and I will get it, cost what it may."*
> *"Then you will degenerate still more, sir."*
> *"Possibly: yet why should I, if I can get sweet fresh pleasure? And I may get it as sweet and fresh as the wild honey the bee gathers on the moor."*
> *"It will sting – it will taste bitter, sir." (14)*

Yet it is part of the wonderful complexity of this book that nobody is more susceptible to Rochester's sexual nature than Jane herself. Rochester's grave and irascible sexuality is filtered entirely through Jane's perception of its power to move her:

> *Most true it is that "beauty is in the eye of the gazer." My master's colourless, olive face, square, massive brow, broad and jetty eyebrows, deep eyes, strong features, firm, grim mouth, – all energy, decision, will,– were not beautiful, according to rule; but they were more than beautiful to me: they were full of an interest, an influence that quite mastered me,– that took my feelings from my own power and fettered them in his. (17)*

In fact, Jane's responsive observation of Rochester at once affirms and contests the conclusions Rochester draws from his equivalent and simultaneous scrutiny – namely, that Jane is an anti-Bertha, whose coolness can restrain any kind of heat, and whose "innocence" and "freshness" can save him from himself. On the contrary, when, at the house party in Miss Ingram's honour, Jane watches Rochester apparently unobserved by him, it seems far from the case that Jane's warm feelings are buried from herself or that she sees Rochester principally as an object of spiritual rescue rather than of sexual desire. Significantly, this passage makes constant intermittent use of the "live" present tense in place of the relative safety and distance of the simple past tense usual for narrative:

> *He comes in last: I am not looking at the arch, yet I see him enter. I try to concentrate my attention... to think only of the work I have in my hands... whereas, I distinctly behold his figure... My eyes were drawn involuntarily to his face; I could not keep their lids under control: they would rise, and the irids would fix on him. I looked, and had acute pleasure in looking, – a precious yet poignant pleasure; pure gold, with a steely point of agony: a pleasure like what the thirst-perishing man might feel who knows the well to which he has crept is poisoned, yet stoops and drinks divine draughts*

nevertheless. (17)

Amid the incipient masochism of Jane's feeling, there is also ruthless and consummate revenge akin to Rochester's casual shooting of his rival for Céline Varens. "Miss Ingram," Jane tells us, equably, "was a mark beneath jealousy: she was too inferior to excite the feeling." Yet this same cool judgement is inseparable here from a kind of vicarious excitement and even sexual fulfilment:

> *I see Mr Rochester turn to Miss Ingram, and Miss Ingram to him; I see her incline her head towards him, till the jetty curls almost touch his shoulder and wave against his cheek; I hear their mutual whisperings... To watch Miss Ingram's efforts at fascinating Mr Rochester; to witness their repeated failure – herself unconscious that they did fail; vainly fancying that each shaft launched, hit the mark... to witness* this, *was to be at once under ceaseless excitation and ruthless restraint.*
>
> *Because, when she failed, I saw how she might have succeeded. Arrows that continually glanced off from Mr Rochester's breast and fell harmless at his feet, might, I knew, if shot by a surer hand, have quivered keen in his proud heart– have called love into his stern eye, and softness into his sardonic face: or, better still, without weapons, a silent conquest might have been won. (18)*

Not only is Jane unambiguously a sexual creature here: she is sexually confident, harbouring no more doubt about her sexual power over Rochester than he possesses about his own power over her. The quasi-submerged sexual character of their relationship is another aspect of its equality, which in turn makes it possible for the novel implicitly to pose fundamental questions about the place of sexuality in loving human relationships, much as Charlotte's sister Emily posed questions about love in *Wuthering Heights*. What does this rash, frenzied, wild, uncontrollable force have to do in a genteel civilised world? Where does it belong? Is it good or evil?

When, for example, Jane douses the fire in Rochester's bedchamber, the meaning of the event is as equivocal as Rochester's meaning to Jane:

> *"I knew... you would do me good in some way, at some time;– I saw it in your eyes when I first beheld you: their expression and smile did not... strike delight to my very inmost heart so for nothing. People talk of natural sympathies; I have heard of good genii... My cherished preserver, good night!"*
>
> *Strange energy was in his voice; strange fire in his look.* (15)

Rochester's belief in Jane's "good" is no more separable at this instant from the "fire" of his feeling for her, than the sexual and religious meanings of fire and water are distinguishable in this whole episode. "Is there a flood?" asks Rochester, at a moment where Gothic, Old Testament and grim black comedy almost madly combine... "No, sir, but there has been a fire." What kind of baptism is this? Is passion a force for life or death? Does it save or damn? "How do you know... How do you know?" Rochester repeatedly asks Jane when she tells him to distrust the lure of sexual degeneracy: "By what instinct do you... distinguish between a fallen seraph of the abyss, and a messenger from the true throne – between a guide and a seducer?" (14). Part of the restless heat of this novel is its struggle with just that question.

For while Rochester continuously associates Jane with a new birth – "While I cannot blight you, you may refresh me," he tells Jane (15) – there is no guarantee that what he finds in Jane is distinct from the "fresh" sexual pleasures to which he is willing to throw himself away. Jane herself never has conviction that the distinction is absolute: immediately following her betrothal to him, she is anxious that he wishes to cast her as "an English Céline Varens" for whom his "love will effervesce in six months, or less" (24).

Nor is Jane convinced that Rochester's influence is not corrupting of the very "good" he needs from her at another level. Directly before she climactically saves Rochester from flames, Jane writes: "I had not forgotten his faults... in my secret soul I knew that his great kindness to me was balanced by unjust severity to many others" (15). Afterwards, when, as observer of his liaison with Blanche Ingram, she admits her own passion for him – "I could not unlove him" – she also fears that she has lost what he himself looks for in her – rational judgement of his shortcomings:

> *I was growing very lenient to my master; I was forgetting all his faults... Now I saw no bad. The sarcasm that had repelled, the harshness that had startled me once, were only like keen condiments in a choice dish: their presence was pungent. (18)*

Yet sexuality in this novel is always potentially an expression, intimation or pursuit of a higher and romantically religious ideal of love, as a union and identity of two souls, obliterating separateness.

> *I feel akin to him... I have something in my brain and heart, in my blood and nerves, that assimilates me mentally to him... Every good, true, vigorous feeling I have, gathers impulsively round him. (17)*

> *"Are you anything akin to me, do you think, Jane?... when you are near me, as now, it is as if I had string somewhere under my left ribs, tightly*

and inextricably knotted to a similar string situated in the corresponding quarter of your little frame." (23)

"I am not talking to you now through the medium of custom, conventionalities, nor even of mortal flesh: – it is my spirit that addresses your spirit: just as if both had passed through the grave, and we stood at God's feet, equal, – as we are!" (23)

"You – you strange – you almost unearthly thing! – I love as my own flesh." (23)

No novel, aside from *Wuthering Heights,* had demonstrated so tenaciously and fearlessly how love might be at once, and perhaps simultaneously, a sexual force, a neurotic obsession and a kind of sacrament. The English novel would have to wait until D.H. Lawrence for anything approaching *Jane Eyre*'s concern with sex as a force which at once connects human beings' primitive biological needs with their yearning for transcendence, and *fulfils* those longings. Rochester's implicit reference to Adam's rib reminds us that sexual love is both a symptom of the Fall and a means to overcome and redeem that same flesh and blood limitation – extending self in another through loving union.

CRITICS ON *JANE EYRE*

"I have been exceedingly moved and pleased by Jane Eyre. *It is a fine book – the man and woman capital – the style very generous and upright... Give my respects and thanks to the author – whose novel is the first English one that I've been able to read for many a day."*

William Makepeace Thackeray (1847)

"Ten years ago we professed an orthodox system of novel-making. Our lovers were humble and devoted – our ladies were beautiful... and the only true love worth having was that reverent, knightly, chivalrous true love which consecrated all woman kind... when suddenly there stole upon the scene... a little fierce incendiary, pale, small, by no means beautiful, doomed to turn the world upside-down... Such was the impetuous little spirit that dashed into our well-ordered world, broke its boundaries and defied its principles – and the most alarming revolution has followed the invasion of Jane Eyre."

Margaret Oliphant (1855)

"Finished Jane Eyre, *which is really a wonderful book, very peculiar in parts, but so powerfully and admirably written, such a fine tone in it, such fine religious feeling, and such beautiful writings. The description of the mysterious maniac's nightly appearances awfully thrilling. Mr Rochester's character a very remarkable one, and Jane Eyre's herself a beautiful one."*

Queen Victoria (1880)

"Charlotte Brontë was surely a marvellous woman. . . . I know no interest more thrilling than that which she has been able to

throw into the characters of Rochester and the governess, in the second volume of Jane Eyre. She lived with those characters, and felt with every fibre of her heart, the longings of the one and the sufferings of the other. And therefore, though the end of the book is weak, and the beginning not very good, I venture to predict that Jane Eyre will be read among English novels when many whose names are now better known shall have been forgotten."

Anthony Trollope (1883)

....

"Brontë does not attempt to solve the problems of human life: she is even unaware that such problems exist: all her force, and it is the more tremendous for being constricted, goes into the assertion, 'I love', 'I hate', 'I suffer'."

Virginia Woolf (1916)

"I find Jane Eyre verging towards pornography ... the strongest instincts have collapsed, and sex has become something slightly obscene, to be wallowed in, but despised. Mr Rochester's sex passion is not 'respectable' till Mr Rochester is burned, blinded, disfigured and reduced to helpless dependence, then, thoroughly humbled and humiliated."

D.H. Lawrence (1929)

....

"In the tightening Victorian world of rigid male self-control, it's significant, surely, how much was kept alive, how much newly affirmed by women novelists like Charlotte Brontë. It wasn't only a case of keeping a woman's world going. On the contrary: in certain vital ways, simply a human world... The Brontë sisters knew a whole structure of repression in their time; knew it and in their own ways broke it with a strength and a courage that puts us all in their debt."

Raymond Williams (1970)

Why does Jane leave Rochester?

"All self-sacrifice is good," wrote George Eliot, on reading *Jane Eyre*, "but one could like it to be in a somewhat nobler cause than that of a diabolical law which chains a man body and soul to a putrefying carcase." Eliot is regretting the influence of social convention – and the legal indissolubility of Rochester's marriage – on Jane's decision to leave Thornfield. More modern readings, such as that of Helene Moglen, for example, suggest her departure is the first decisive and "crucial step" in Jane's feminist independence – and can be seen as continuous with her resistance to Rochester's lavish plans for transforming her from governess to wife ("I can never bear being dressed like a doll by Mr Rochester... I will be myself" (24)). Certainly, it is tempting to see Jane's motivation as broadly socio-political – whether it is a prim falling back on convention or a bold feminist stance – since, emotionally, Jane has every reason to stay with Rochester.

First, there is the fact, as obvious as it is primary, that Jane loves Rochester. "I love Thornfield," she cries, when, earlier in the novel, she believes he will marry Blanche Ingram.

> *"I love it, because I have lived in it a full and delightful life... with an original, a vigorous, and expanded mind. I have known you, Mr Rochester; and it strikes me with terror and anguish to feel I absolutely must be torn from you for ever. I see the necessity of departure; and it feels like looking on the necessity of death." (23)*

Second, without him, she will be, terribly, alone in the world once more, no more than "Jane Eyre... a cold, solitary girl again, her life... pale; her prospects... desolate... Where was her life?" (26). Third, Jane *forgives* Rochester – instantly, "at the moment, and on the spot".

> *There was such deep remorse in his eye, such true pity in his tone, such manly energy in his manner... such unchanged love in his whole look and mien – I forgave him all... at my heart's core. (27)*

Fourth, *he* loves *her*.

> *"Every atom of your flesh is as dear to me as my own: in pain and sickness it would still be dear. Your mind is my treasure, and if it were broken, it would be my treasure still." (27)*

Furthermore, he can provide for her materially, in a situation at least as respectable as that of a governess. As Rochester points out, Jane has "neither relatives nor acquaintances whom [she] need fear" by living with him in the South of France (27). Finally, in leaving Rochester, she risks abandoning him to the dissolute life from which she has always, from their first meeting, assiduously dissuaded him:

> *"It seems to me, that if you tried hard, you would in time find it possible to become what you yourself would approve... if from this day you began with resolution to correct your thoughts and actions."* (14)

But these very motivations for remaining with Rochester, precisely in so far as they are *compelling*, are experienced by Jane as *temptations* which she must severely and repeatedly school herself to resist. And it is important to distinguish Jane's resistance here from her habitual repression of emotion in relation to Rochester. When she believes he is Blanche Ingram's suitor, for example, she "endeavoured to bring back with a strict hand such [thoughts and feelings] as had been straying... Reason... show[ed] how I had rejected the real and rabidly devoured the ideal" (16). This distinction is especially necessary given that the two phenomena – resistance, denial – seem so closely

Opposite: Panel from front cover of Look and Learn *no. 179 (19 June 1965)*

related here. Jane's first reaction to the revelation of Bertha's existence is to shut herself "into her own room, and fast the bolt, that none might intrude". At one level, this is indeed a retreat from sensuality into mind, in order to locate therein an anti-Romantic, anti-Gothic, determined rationalism, even in the midst of self-defeat:

> *I felt weak and tired. I leaned my arms on a table, and my head dropped on them. And now I thought: till now I had only heard, seen, moved – followed up and down where I was led or dragged – watched event rush on event, disclosure open beyond disclosure: but now, I thought... From his presence I must go: that I perceived well. (26)*

There is more, however, to that "I thought" than the triumph of reason over feeling. For the very separateness of mind and feeling remains a critical problem for Jane here.

> *I asked, "What am I to do?"*
>
> *But the answer my mind gave – "Leave Thornfield at once"– was so prompt, so dread, that I stopped my ears: I said, I could not bear such words now... that I must leave him decidedly, instantly, entirely, is intolerable. I cannot do it.*
>
> *But, then, a voice within me averred that I could do it; and foretold that I should do it. I*

wrestled with my own resolution: I wanted to be
weak that I might avoid the awful passage of
further suffering I saw laid out for me. (27)

The first person "I" in this passage is not strictly
singular. Sometimes (as in "I stopped my ears", "I
could not bear", "I cannot do it") the "I" is not
synonymous with those other first-person entities
– "my mind", "my own resolution", "a voice within
me" – and sometimes it is ("I should do it", "I
could do it"). The big test for Jane, in the first
instance, is not primarily that of locating the right
verb – "I felt" and "I thought" – but locating the
right "I", the right "voice" or "inward power"
(27). And this challenge has to be undertaken not
from within the relatively protected mental space
of her own room and mind but in the context of
the physical presence and power of Rochester. Her
resolution has to "wrestle" now not only with her
own "weak" inner voices, but with the passionate
strength of Rochester's own. She must withstand
him when he makes a direct appeal to her love:

"Jane! Jane!" he said – in such an accent of bitter
sadness, it thrilled along every nerve I had; "you
don't love me, then? It was only my station, and the
rank of my wife, that you valued? Now... you recoil
from my touch as if I were some toad or ape."
*   These words cut me... I was so tortured by a*
sense of remorse at thus hurting his feelings, I

*could not control the wish to drop balm where I
had wounded. (27)*

She must continue to resist when he tries to
render her very strengths a source of weakness –
"Jane," he asks, of all things, as she strives to locate
her own judgement, "will you hear reason?"– and,
again, when the sheer heat of his raging sexual
presence becomes a very real threat to them both:

*His voice and hand quivered; his large nostrils
dilated; his eyes blazed... "Jane, I am not a gentle-
tempered man – you forget that: I am not long-
enduring; I am not cool and dispassionate. Out of
pity to me and yourself, put your finger on my
pulse, feel how it throbs, and – beware!" (27)*

*His fury was wrought to the highest... he crossed
the floor and seized my arm, and grasped my
waist. He seemed to devour me with his flaming
glance: physically, I felt, at the moment, powerless
as stubble exposed to the draught and glow of a
furnace. (27)*

The biblical evocation here – "Therefore as the
fire devoureth the stubble, and the flame
consumeth the chaff, so their root shall be as
rottenness, and their blossom shall go up as dust"
(Isaiah, 5:25) – is highly significant. For the
greatest temptation of all is a religious one: the

very real possibility that by staying with him, she might save him from himself, where, by abandoning him, she leaves him to the devil:

> "After a youth and manhood, passed half in unutterable misery and half in dreary solitude, I have for the first time found what I can truly love – I have found you. You are my sympathy – my better self – my good angel..."
>
> I was experiencing an ordeal: a hand of fiery iron grasped my vitals. Terrible moment: full of struggle, blackness, burning! Not a human being that ever lived could wish to be loved better than I was: and him who thus loved me I absolutely worshipped: and I must renounce love and idol. (27)

> While he spoke my very Conscience and Reason turned traitors against me, and charged me with crime in resisting him. They spoke almost as loud as Feeling: and that clamoured wildly. "Oh, comply!" it said. "Think of his misery, think of his danger – look at his state when left alone: remember his headlong nature; consider the recklessness following on despair – soothe him, save him; love him: tell him you love him and will be his. Who in the world cares for you? or who will be injured by what you do?" (27)

The hardest thing of all at this moment, "with

[her] veins running fire, and [her] heart beating faster than [she] can count its throbs" – when Conscience itself accuses her of selfishness and it seems even *morally* wrong to leave Rochester – is for Jane to say those crucial four words: "I care for myself." "Rather than being a rigid moralist after the zealots of the book, Jane bases her ultimate morality on a standard relative to the individual," says John Maynard. "It is not that she couldn't disagree with convention, only that she disqualifies herself to do so under her present passion. Like Bertha, she is insane when sexually aroused, 'insane – quite insane'."

But Jane's words are not the triumph of reason over passion. On the contrary, this is the first of two dramatically crucial instances in the latter portion of the novel where thought and feeling, being and doing, "inward power" and external identity, "I" and "myself", powerfully and incontrovertibly coalesce. "The more solitary, the more friendless, the more unsustained I am, the more I will respect myself" (27). "For someone as socially isolated as Jane, the self is all one has," writes Terry Eagleton. "'Self-possession' comes to assume a meaning deeper than the coolly impenetrable... it suggests also a nurturing and hoarding of the self." But Jane has the luxury neither of being "cool" nor of privately "hoarding" herself. The very fact that her respect for herself remains an inward law, not an externally enforceable one – the fact that she might so easily "get away with" giving up on herself – means that these pressures preserve their influence up to the very moment of her departure:

> *He released me from his clutch and only looked at me. The look was far worse to resist than the frantic strain... I had dared and baffled his fury; I must elude his sorrow. (27)*

> *I would have got past Mr Rochester's chamber without a pause; but my heart momentarily stopping its beat at the threshold, my foot was forced to stop also... There was a heaven – a temporary heaven – in this room for me, if I chose. (27)*

Moreover, once she has left, there is no feminist sense of emancipation, no "self-possession" in any sense, nothing that feels like an achievement. There is only loneliness and longing – "with agony I thought of what I had left... I longed to be his" – and the continuous fears for Rochester, which will never leave her, just because *she* has left *him* to make his own way:

> *His self-abandonment – far worse than my abandonment – how it goaded me! It was a barbed arrow-head in my breast... I abhorred myself. I had no solace from self-approbation: none even*

from self-respect. I had injured – wounded – left
my master. I was hateful in my own eyes. (27)

This is heroism that has no glamour of the heroic: a highly charged instance of romantic love that has nothing conventionally romantic about it. No earlier novel had so fearlessly placed such existential and spiritual tests inside highly charged sexual ones, or found bravery amid profound and intolerable self-loathing. This impure mix of levels of experience was to become the hallmark of high Victorian realism for which, for all its Romantic heritage, *Jane Eyre* set a template and a standard.

Why does Jane return to Rochester?

The portion of the novel which recounts Jane's time as a parish schoolteacher at Morton, and her connection with the Rivers family, is often neglected, especially in film or television adaptations, as being irrelevant or at best secondary to the central love story. But this episode does not simply fill in gaps in the plot or delay Jane's climactic return to Rochester. It offers a crucial perspective on and prelude to that final reunion. "I will keep the law given by God," says Jane to Rochester when she breaks from him definitively. In the next move of the novel she encounters the Reverend St John Rivers, an external embodiment of those very "laws and principles" on the strength of which Jane has rejected Rochester. Recounting his own experience of love's "delirium and delusion", St John tells Jane:

"I love Rosamond Oliver so wildly – with all the intensity, indeed, of a first passion, the object of which is exquisitely beautiful, graceful, and fascinating – I experience at the same time a calm, unwarped consciousness, that she would not make me a good wife; that she is not the partner suited to me; that I should discover this within a year after marriage; and that to twelve months' rapture would succeed a lifetime of regret. This I know." (32)

St John offers an alternative to Rochester, both structurally as an opposing character type, and personally as a potential mate for Jane. "Restless", "eager" (29), "troubled by insatiate yearnings", by whose sermons "the heart was thrilled, the mind astonished", (30), St John is a man of passion who yet can exercise just the kind of judgement in respect of his sensual appetite – "This I know" – which might have saved Rochester from his disastrous marriage to Bertha. Moreover, even before St John's literal kinship to Jane is disclosed, there is a strong sense of likeness.

> *I was sure St John Rivers – pure-lived, conscientious, zealous as he was – had not yet found that peace of God which passeth all understanding: he had no more found it, I thought, than had I; with my concealed and racking regrets*

DREAMS AND VISIONS

"Presentiments are strange things!... one mystery to which humanity has not yet found the key" (21). Two explicit "presentiments" or "visionary experiences" occur to Jane in the novel. The first is the apparition of her mother's spirit urging her to leave Rochester. The second is the "telepathic" summons from Rochester calling her back to him. While both have convincing psychological explanations, they each occur in moonlight, "an aesthetic staple [which] reveals an author groping for... a reality beyond the confines of everyday reality, toward an interplay of private consciousness and mysterious forces at work in the universe", says Robert B. Heilman.

The first of these explicitly recalls Jane's childhood trauma while living with the Reeds:

> *I dreamt I lay in the red-room at Gateshead... The light that long ago had struck me... seemed glidingly to mount the wall... the roof resolved to clouds, high and dim; the gleam was such as the moon imparts to vapours she is about to sever. I watched her come... She*

for my broken idol and Elysium... which possessed
me and tyrannised over me ruthlessly. (30)

And St John directly mirrors her own history when he says:

"It is hard work to control the workings of
inclination, and turn the bent of nature: but that it
may be done, I know from experience. God has

broke forth as never moon yet
burst from cloud... not a
moon, but a white human
form shone in the azure... It
spoke, to my spirit:
immeasurably distant was
the tone, yet so near, it
whispered in my heart –
"My daughter, flee
temptation!"
"Mother, I will."

In the red room vision, the very love Jane so craved was as alienating and fearful a presence – a "preternatural comfort" proceeding from the spirit of her dead Uncle Reed – as her own "phantom" self. In one recurrent vision at Thornfield, Jane dreams of an infant whom she comforts, hushes and plays with in loving "companionship" – a "baby-phantom" which recalls the Gateshead nightmare directly before Jane is physically summoned to the past to see her dying Aunt Reed.

The infant reappears in two further dreams on the eve of Jane's wedding. In the first, Jane is "following the windings of an unknown road", in "total obscurity", "burdened" with a cold, shivering, wailing child, and seeing, so she believes, Rochester on the road a long way ahead. In the second, still carrying the unknown child, which weighs her down and impedes her progress, she finds Thornfield (prophetically enough) "a dreary ruin", and hears Rochester riding away. As she climbs a wall to catch a last glimpse of him, she loses *given us, in a measure, the power to make our own fate." (31)*

When his sister Diana warns Jane that "St John looks quiet... but he hides a fever in his vitals... in some things he is inexorable as death" (30), this is consonant not only with Jane's own assessment – "With all his firmness and self-control... [he]

---

balance and the child rolls away.

The child, say Gilbert and Gubar, seems to represent the burden of Jane's past, just as Bertha stands (more literally) for Rochester's. "Until [Jane] reaches... maturity, independence, true equality with Rochester (and therefore in a sense with the rest of the world) she is doomed to follow her orphaned alter ego everywhere." Thus, at the critical moment of test, when Jane refuses to live with Rochester while Bertha remains his wife, Jane's decision to "care" for her future effectively frees her from her past, allowing the child finally to be absorbed into the adult self. Saying "I will" to the only spirit guide – angel? or ghost? – who might

care for her more than herself, replaces the "I will" of the marriage vow, not regressively, but progressively, therefore.

Jane hears Rochester's voice – calling "'Jane! Jane! Jane!'... wildly, eerily, urgently, where or whence for ever impossible to know" – at the moment when, pressed now to accept St John's proposal of marriage, she entreats Heaven to guide her (35). She leaves it to "the reader" to judge whether the cry she hears is "the effect of excitement", inviting her interlocutor to recall how Jane once told Rochester (on his return to Thornfield on the eve of their wedding): "I beheld you in imagination so near me, I scarcely missed your actual presence" (25).

But Jane's own judgement

locks every feeling and pang within – expresses, confesses, imparts nothing" (32) – but with Jane herself, of course. She alone in this novel can rival St John for an uncompromising energy of will, capable of restraining full frustrated responsiveness to the limitation which that very energy of principle determines. Desolate, degraded and demeaned by her new station in life,

of the event is clear, and is startlingly vindicated by Rochester's corresponding account, when they are reunited, of having heard Jane's answering words – "Where are you?" – "on the wind" (III, 11). "Down superstition!" she commands her own scepticism. "This is not thy deception, nor thy witchcraft: it is the work of nature. She was roused and did – no miracle – but her best" (III, 9). "Nature" hovers ambiguously here – as it does frequently throughout the novel – between human, environmental and providential reference, seeming neither to preclude the possibility of psychic delusion, nor to accept that explanation.

Henry James's famous distinction between the art of the realist, which is "tied to the earth" and the art of the "romancer" which "cuts the cable" to pursue uncharted experience, does not really hold in the case of *Jane Eyre*, where realism and romance alike seem to seek and disclose some deeper reality. Robert B. Heilman writes:

> *In her flair for the surreal, in her plunging into feeling that is without status in the ordinary world of the novel, Charlotte discovers a new dimension... [a] rehabilitation of the extra-rational, which is the historical office of Gothic... no longer oriented in marvellous circumstance but moving deeply into the lesser-known realities of human life •*

Jane still can say, "inexorably":

> *Which is better? – To have surrendered to*
> *temptation; listened to passion; made no painful*
> *effort – no struggle... to be slave in a fool's paradise*
> *in Marseilles – fevered with delusive bliss one*
> *hour– suffocating with the bitterest tears of*
> *remorse and shame the next – or to be a village*
> *schoolmistress, free and honest, in a breezy*
> *mountain nook in the healthy heart of England?*
> *(31)*

What Jane finds in Rivers, then, is a version of her own self. Where Bertha embodies Jane's displaced sexuality, in Rivers the austerity Jane has cherished as her inward guardian now confronts her externally. Moreover, it hurts her emotionally – "She looks sensible, but not at all handsome... Ill or well, she would always be plain" is St John's cold assessment of her (29) – as much as Bertha threatened to do physically. Structurally, St John is more a foil to Bertha than to Rochester, pitting against her animal instinct his inverse (wrong) model of pure rationalism: "I am simply, in my original state – stripped of that bloodbleached robe with which Christianity covers human deformity – a cold, hard, ambitious man... Reason, and not Feeling, is my guide" (32). But for all his fierce zeal, stern stoicism and loveless rigidity – "a statue instead of a man" (29) – St John does represent one of the central problems of the book: "He could not bind all that he had in his nature– the rover, the aspirant, the poet, the priest – in the limits of a single passion" (32).

The entire novel might be understood as a study in looking for a "home" for energies which exceed the capacity of the human frame to hold them. "Propensities and principles must be reconciled by some means," says St John – while the novel seems to say, from Brocklehurst onwards, "not by this means" (repression). Nor can it recommend the promiscuous expending of energies which characterises the first two-thirds of the book. To find her own means, Jane must undergo another trial.

For St John does not simply represent a corrective to Jane but also an *enticement*. He offers a serious alternative life for her, precisely because he offers full sympathetic fellowship in the ontological *problem**, as well as proposing a practical *solution*:

> *"I read it in your eye: it is not of that description which promises the maintenance of an even tenor in life... I mean, that human affections and sympathies have a most powerful hold on you. I am sure you cannot long be content to pass your*

---

* That is to say, a concern with the nature of being (in this case, Jane's identity).

*leisure in solitude, and to devote your working
hours to a monotonous labour wholly void of
stimulus; any more than I can be content... to live
here buried in morass, pent in with mountain – my
nature, that God gave me, contravened; my
faculties heaven-bestowed, paralysed – made
useless." (30)*

*"When our energies seem to demand a sustenance
they cannot get – when our will strains after a path
we may not follow – we need neither starve from
inanition, nor stand still in despair: we have but to
seek another nourishment for the mind, as strong
as the forbidden food it longed to taste – and
perhaps purer; and to hew out for the adventurous
foot a road as direct and broad as the one Fortune
has blocked up against us, if rougher than it." (31)*

When St John asks her to leave for India with him
as helpmeet in the fulfilment of his missionary
purpose, it is never inconceivable that he is
offering salvation – a pastor recalling his
wandering lamb (35). Jane is guided to Marsh
End, after all, by a single light when, burdened
with a life she believes valueless, she asks
Providence to "direct me". When she says, "I can
but die... Let me try to wait His will in silence", she
hears St John's voice "close at hand", very literally

Opposite: Charlotte Gainsbourg and William Hurt in Franco Zeffirelli's 1996 film

her saviour (28). She might lament that as

> *daily [I] wished more to please him... I felt daily*
> *more and more that I must disown half my nature,*
> *stifle half my faculties, wrest my tastes from their*
> *original bent, force myself to the adoption of*
> *pursuits for which I had no natural vocation...*
> *(34)*

Yet, for all this sense that they are unnaturally matched, he is still "*half* her nature", even so, in more than just familial brotherhood. And she has no one and nothing else.

> *In leaving England, I should leave a loved but*
> *empty land – Mr Rochester is not there: and if he*
> *were, what is, what can that ever be to me? My*
> *business is to live without him now: I must seek*
> *another interest in life to replace the one lost: is not*
> *the occupation he now offers me truly the most*
> *glorious man can adopt or God assign? (34)*

It is precisely the fact that it is the religious life which offers itself as temptation here, which makes it all the more heroic that Jane resists that possibility as a fundamental betrayal of her existential needs: "Alas! If I join St John... if I go to India, I go to premature death":

> *"I wish I could make you see how much my mind is*

at this moment like a rayless dungeon, with one
shrinking fear fettered in its depths – the fear of
being persuaded by you to attempt what I cannot
accomplish." (34)

I felt how – if I were his wife – this good man, pure
as the deep sunless source, could soon kill me;
without drawing from my veins a single drop of
blood, or receiving on his own crystal conscience
the faintest stain of crime. (35)

"If I were to marry you, you would kill me, you are
killing me now… To do as you wish me, would I
begin to think, be almost equivalent to committing
suicide." (35)

It is a remarkable moment in an essentially
religious novel, that the true act of faith is the
refusal of the formal religious life: "I will give the
missionary my energies – it is all he wants – but
not myself" (34).

What does the ending of *Jane Eyre* mean?

For many readers, "the blackened ruin" which Jane finds when she returns to Thornfield, and the blinded, scorched and charred Rochester she seeks out at Ferndean, represent the vanquishing of the novel's sexual energies. "Mr Rochester's sex passion is not 'respectable'," said D.H. Lawrence, "till Mr Rochester is burned, blinded, disfigured and reduced to helpless dependence. Then, thoroughly humbled and humiliated, it may be merely admitted." Later 20th-century critics also regarded Rochester's mutilation and blindness as a sort of "symbolic castration". A "sightless Samson", shorn of masculine strength, is how Rochester first appears to Jane. "Much of *Jane Eyre*'s rather nasty power as a novel depends upon its author's attitude towards men, which is nobly sadistic as befits a disciple of Byron," writes the American academic, Harold Bloom.

For feminist critics, on the other hand, the overcoming of the novel's fire is chiefly regrettable in terms of what it means for the heroine. For all her rebellious energy, Jane is at last reduced to the role of desexualised submissive servant and to the duties of the stereotypical wife which she had once regarded as anathema. Indeed, in Helene Moglen's view, "it is not a lover [Rochester] requires, but a mother who can offer him again the gift of life". Virginal Jane "has been magically transformed – without the mediation of sexual contact – into the noble figure of the nurturing mother". In other words, the novel's close constitutes a standard Victorian ending, where all non-conformist elements are restrained or tamed, and the female heroine reverts to patriarchal type.

Yet Jane returns to Rochester as a woman of family, wealth and means, not as his dependant. She is the capable adult who dispels Rochester's morbid delusion that she is not his "living Jane" but "an empty mockery" – "'Ah, this is practical – this is real,' he cried" (37) – and who counters his vulnerable fear – "Will she not depart as suddenly as she came?" – with "a commonplace, practical reply, out of the train of his own disturbed ideas... the most reassuring [for] this frame of mind". It is also *she* who now taunts *him* with the possibility of a rival: "'This St John then is your cousin?'... (*Aside*) 'Damn him!' – (*To me*) 'Did you like him, Jane?'" And it is now Jane who virtually proposes to *Rochester*: "'Cease to look so desolate, my dear master; you shall not be left desolate so long as I live." Jane's continuing use of the terms "sir" and "master" bespeak a tender tact towards Rochester's condition, even as they remind us of the degree to which the lovers' positions are now reversed.

She is now his guide in life. "I was then his

vision as I am now his right hand." When Jane famously announces "Reader, I married him", at the opening of the final chapter, the key emphasis falls not upon the event of marriage as a sacrifice to convention, but, on the contrary, upon the first-person assertion of a chosen destiny. (The sentence is not "Reader, we were married.") In this interpretation, the close of the novel respects a formal, not a socio-political expectation, for it represents, in classic *Bildungsroman* mode, the "essential epilogue to [Jane's] pilgrimage toward selfhood", as Sandra Gilbert and Susan Gubar put it.

But that selfhood is still defined as part of a loving union, in which Rochester is also changed.

> *"Who can tell what a dark, dreary, hopeless life I have dragged on for months past... a very delirium of desire to hold my Jane again. Yes: for her restoration I longed, far more than for that of my lost sight." (37)*

> *"You think me... an irreligious dog: but... of late, Jane – only of late – I began to see and acknowledge the hand of God in my doom... to experience remorse, repentance." (37)*

Rochester's transformation is not so much that of a man emasculated and impotent, but of one who, by losing sight of his overweaning masculinity, is able to see himself more clearly. His words – "I did wrong" – have the force of blinded Gloucester in *King Lear* when he says: "I stumbled when I saw." Indeed the "subjugation of [Rochester's] vigorous spirit to a corporeal infirmity" is almost Lear-like in its power to move Jane – "just as if a royal eagle, chained to a perch, should be forced to entreat a sparrow to become its purveyor" (37) – since she to him is a Cordelia in whose return he can hardly believe: "Oh, you are indeed there, my sky-lark!... You are not gone: not vanished?"

But the resurrection Jane offers is real not illusory because she comes back not as a daughter figure or mere helpmeet, but as a sexual mate for whom Rochester's potency is never in doubt: that, after all, is what her continued use of the term "master" really means. "I am no better than the old, lightning-struck chestnut tree in Thornfield orchard"; "You are no ruin, sir – no lightning -struck tree: you are green and vigorous. Plants will grow about your roots, whether you ask them or not" (37).

For many, the ending of the novel has strong religious significance in which Ferndean – a withdrawn natural world ("deep-buried in a wood... all interwoven stem... dense summer foliage" (37), secluded from society, where the lovers find spiritual identity – is a kind of Eden restored. When, in the final chapter, first and third person singular become mutually interchangeable – "I am my husband's life as fully as he is mine"; "I know no weariness of my Edward's society: he knows none of mine" – and then resolve into a marital syntax – "any more than we each do of the pulsation of the heart that beats in our separate bosoms… we are ever together" – the very grammar of their relationship signals perfect union. In a sense, at Ferndean, the political and religious meanings of Jane and Rochester's relationship converge: they achieve a marriage of souls and an egalitarian, non-exploitative partnership.

For other readers, the close is more expressive of the Fall than of Paradise regained, not least because of Ferndean's questionable paradisial credentials. Once deemed too "ineligible and insalubrious" even for Bertha's residence, it is "a desolate spot", with house and grounds decaying, uninhabited and inaccessible, and its wild growth characterised by autumnal ripeness. Not only is this an inauspicious setting for new beginnings: it seems tacitly to admit that the achievement of Jane and Rochester's relationship is only possible outside the conventions of a fallen world. Certainly by closing the entire novel with the austere example of St John's single, missionary, religious life, Brontë is suggesting that the choices are few and austere for those who wish to live a meaningful life on earth. St John's life is offered as

Jane's counter-narrative, her might-have-been life, and, it seems, the only possible alternative for her, as a person to whom life is a serious matter. If she has chosen more the "human" than the "divine" path, the novel leaves us in no doubt that this way is no less stringent or exacting.

NATURAL AND SUPERNATURAL

No tie holds me to human society at this moment – not a charm or hope calls me where my fellow-creatures are – none that saw me would have a kind thought or a good wish for me. I have no relative but the universal mother, Nature: I will seek her breast and ask her repose. (28)

Having left Rochester for ever as she believes, Jane comes thus "home" to nature, finding, in extremis, the primary kinship which has sustained her throughout her experience of unsatisfactory or equivocal homes from childhood to adulthood. Landscape and plant life are indeed kindred parts of her own self, moods, and needs. Looking out upon a snowstorm at Lowood, Jane relishes the tumult as belonging to her own turbulent nature, and even in this providing a strange surrogate parentage:

Probably, if I had lately left a good home and kind parents, this would have been the hour when I should most keenly have regretted the separation: that wind would then have saddened my heart; this obscure chaos would have disturbed my peace: as it was I derived from both a strange excitement, and reckless and feverish, I wished the wind to howl more wildly, the gloom to deepen to darkness, and the confusion to rise to clamour. (6)

Nature is a true beneficent influence, not simply a subjectivist "fallacy". After the privations and hardships of her first winter, Jane discovers – "free, unwatched and alone" – that "a great pleasure, which only the horizon bounded, lay all outside the high and spiked walls of our garden". Her liberated Romantic imagination and artist's eye is nourished equally by nature's sublime "noble summits" as by its vigorous growth and warmth of colour: "vegetation... sprang up profusely... and made a strange ground-sunshine out of the wealth of its wild primrose plants." (6)

At Thornfield, natural life ministers to the growing love between Jane and Rochester as tangibly as it takes part in the love affair between Tess and Angel Clare in Thomas Hardy's *Tess of the D'Urbervilles*. In a "stripped" winter landscape of "utter solitude and leafless repose", in which the earth prepares to begin again, Jane's Wordsworthian contemplative calm – "in the absolute hush I could hear... thin murmurs of life. My ear too felt the flow of currents" – is broken in upon by the "rude noise" (12) of Rochester's first arrival. The new beginning, even as it brings an end to the solitary self-sufficiencies of Jane's childhood and virgin womanhood, is as alarming as it is sexually promising.

When, later, Jane returns from her visit to the dying Mrs Reed, on another evening, but in summertime now, with haymakers at work and leafy and flowery branches "shooting" across the path, Rochester's welcome gives back the calm he had stolen: his "words were balm... he had spoken of Thornfield as my home" (22). Nature's seasonal cycle of beginnings and endings, the sequence of clear daylight dispelling the secrets of the night, calm replacing storm, reality putting vision to flight, is one of the basic rhythms of the book.

While the presence of organic nature is another inheritance from the Romantics, the novel also passes on that Romantic tradition through the lineage of the novel. At such moments Jane is as much a prototype Hardyesque heroine as an embodiment of female Romanticism. But what makes this a mid-Victorian rather than a resolutely secular *fin de siècle* novel is the continued power and orthodoxy of the religious significance of nature in *Jane Eyre*.

The novel's staple elemental imagery, for example, gains amplitude and dimension from its mythical and biblical origins. Fire, traditionally the source of heat, light and life itself (stolen from the gods and given to humans, in the Promethean myth), is also an avenging scourge, consuming and destructive, and both associative extremes are powerfully exploited in *Jane Eyre*. Throughout the novel, water, too, is multiply suggestive of death and rebirth. In the bitter hour after the abandonment of the marriage service, "the waters came into my soul", says Jane (quoting the Psalms). "I sank in deep mire: I felt no standing; I came into deep waters; the floods overflowed me" (26). Yet, in the terrible wandering in voluntary exile which ensues, it is from "the rain... wetting me afresh to the skin... my yet living flesh shudder[ing] at its chilling influence" that, Jane tells us, "I rose ere long", as if in involuntary resurrection.

Significantly, it is on a "fresh" spring morning washed by "April showers" that Rochester leads Jane to the orchard after the night of Bertha's attack on Mason ("Come where there is some freshness... here all is real and sweet and pure"), and asks of "good and bright" Jane – "all fresh, healthy, without soil and without taint" – whether he too might not be renewed and restored, in spite of his errors, by her good offices:

"Is the wandering and sinful, but now rest-seeking and repentant man, justified in daring the world's opinion, in order to attach to him for ever, this gentle, gracious, genial stranger: thereby securing his own peace of mind and regeneration?" (20)

One of the most significant biblical allusions occurs in the climactic proposal scene, where the "blooming" orchard on midsummer eve – a night of intense fruition of nature and feeling – is now explicitly "Eden-like". The very moment of consummation and apparent redemption – "I ask you to pass through life at my side – to be my second self and best earthly companion" – signals the imminence of the Fall. The ruin by lightning (heaven's fire) of the chestnut tree is as providentially judgemental as it is (in recalling Coleridge's poem "Cristabel") unmistakably Romantic.

Jane Eyre, says David Lodge, is remarkable for the way it asserts a rigorous and demanding biblical moral code in a fictional world that is not God-centred but concerned with individuality and subjectivity. While references to the orthodox idea of hellfire are largely satirised in *Jane Eyre* (in Brocklehurst, for example):

> the sanctions of Old Testament morality – punishment by fire and water, destitution, exile, solitariness – are still very much in evidence on both the literal and metaphorical levels. But the symbolic art of the novel presents them as extensions of the individual consciousness. The relationship of Jane and Rochester appears to us not as something which, according to its lawfulness or unlawfulness, will bring punishment or reward from an external source, but which contains within itself possibilities of fulfilment and destruction.

EARTH, WATER, AIR AND FIRE

In his famous and definitive essay in *The Language of Fiction*, David Lodge explores the extensive use of imagery drawn from the four elements to characterise Jane's experience. Lodge proposes that the network of images constitutes a core "system" of elemental reference, which shifts flexibly and constantly between the prosaic, and the poetic and symbolic. In this way, the novel constantly modulates between

> on the one hand, writing which is firmly realistic and literal, keenly sensitive to common emotions and sensations, insisting on the value... of ordinary human affection; and on the other hand, writing which is visionary... evocative of heightened states of feeling, insisting on the value of self-fulfilment... conducted at an extraordinary pitch of imaginative perception.

Jane Eyre's own name is caught up in the elemental network, punningly invoking both "air" and "ire" (the latter of which results in Jane's banishment to the red room where the word is metaphorically indistinguishable from "fire" – "forlorn depression fell damp on my decaying ire" (3)). Fire, traditionally chief among the elements, dominates the novel too, especially as it is contrasted with its lower-order rivals, often present or invoked in their harsh manifestations as rock, wind and ice. The burning of Rochester's bed literalises the association of fire with sexual energy and passionate emotion throughout the book. As "life, fire, feeling" are synonymous for Jane (12), so, for Rochester, "to live... is to stand on a crater crust which may crack and spue fire any day" (20). As Jane is "fire-spirit" (24) to Rochester – "You are cold because you are alone; no contact strikes the fire from you that is in you" (18) – so Jane beholds "ascending heart-fire" in Rochester's features (26) and longs "to dare" the "strange depth... volcanic abyss" which she divines in his eye (18).

In St John, by contrast, she finds a being "cold as an iceberg" (37), not "flesh but marble", who casts "a freezing spell" and salutes with "ice kisses" (36). These associations and counter-associations help define the "choice" which faces Jane, of Rochester or St John, as one of primal existential seriousness – passion or emotion, fire or ice, life or death – rather than simply a matter of most suitable romantic partner: "Reader, do you know as I do," Jane asks when St John re-urges his offer of marriage, "what terror those cold people can put into the ice of their questions? How much of the fall of the avalanche is in their anger? of the breaking up of the frozen sea of their displeasure?" (37).

Yet the simple ordinary home-fire is one key to the power of these more dramatically antagonistic formal patterns. A naturalistic staple of the novel's domestic milieu, fire is also figuratively associated with human warmth, vitality and friendship – qualities which the hearth-fire seems almost literally to engender. Amid the inhospitable cold and bleakness of Lowood, Miss Temple's "good", "brilliant" fire "kindled" the powers in Helen Burns's mind, the influence of which "glowed" in her cheek and "shone" in her eye (8). Jane's first intense conversations with Rochester are warmed by "a large fire red and clear", and "a festal breadth of light", in which setting Rochester's eyes "sparkled" as he "received the light of the fire on his granite-hewn features", and his "frigid and rigid temper" relaxed (14). By contrast, Jane finds St John at the fireside "too often a cold cumbrous column, gloomy and out of place" (8). The ritual of fire-making accompanies all significant domestic events of homecoming and reunion (including Rochester's first homecoming and the Rivers sisters' return to Marsh End).

Moreover, throughout the book home-fires, present or extinguished, real and metaphorical, are a significant point of reference in Jane's struggle towards acceptance and domestic happiness. Her first appearance in the novel is marked by her exclusion from the Reed family fireside circle, imaginatively immersed in the Arctic landscape of Bewick's *History of British Birds*: "forlorn regions of dreary space... frost and snow... firm fields of ice... glazed in Alpine heights above heights". Jane looks from her secluded window-seat upon "the dreary November day... a pale blank of mist and cloud... wet lawn and storm-beat shrub, with ceaseless rain sweeping away wildly" (1). On the eve of her aborted wedding, she tells Rochester how, in his absence, "as it grew dark, the wind rose... wild and high... the sight of the empty chair and fireless hearth chilled me" (25), and, when the marriage service has been prevented, Jane figures her "pale" life and prospects as "spread waste, wild and white as pine forests in wintry Norway": "A Christmas frost had come at midsummer; a white December storm had whirled over June" (26).

At the end of the novel, Jane is reunited with Rochester under an aspect which is equivalent to that of the novel's opening – "an evening marked by characteristics of sad sky, cold gale, and continued, small, penetrating rain" (26) – yet which is now reversed by Jane's reviving of the "neglected handful of fire", a practical and ordinary action which promises recovery at every level, including Rochester's sight: "Yes, with the right eye I see a glow– a ruddy haze."

The poetry of *Jane Eyre*, says Lodge, grows naturally out of the literal life of the novel.

The interior landscape of Jane's emotions is no less real than the landscape she look[s] out on and "wanders" within... The reverse is also true: literal phrases that are potentially clichés – "icy cold", "good fire" – are re-charged with expressive force by echoing the novel's daring tropes.

The deployment of figurative elemental power, at these different levels of prosaic and visionary existence, helps unite and contain these orders of experience within a single literary structure which also "persuade[s] us that they can co-exist in a single consciousness and that they can be reconciled", however unevenly.

1816 Charlotte Brontë born. Jane Austen's *Emma* published.

1817 Branwell Brontë born.

1818 Emily Brontë born.

1820 Anne Brontë born. Family moves to Haworth Parsonage in Yorkshire.

1821 Charlotte's mother dies of cancer.

1824 Charlotte's older sisters, Maria and Elizabeth, go to Clergy Daughters School, Cowan Bridge, followed by Charlotte and her younger sister, Emily.

1825 Maria and Elizabeth brought home to die of tuberculosis.

1826 Patrick, Charlotte's father, brings home wooden soldiers which stimulate his children's early writings.

1837 Victoria becomes Queen.

1839 Charlotte becomes a governess (for two months) and refuses two marriage proposals.

1841 Charlotte and Emily persuade their Aunt Branwell to pay for them to go to Brussels to perfect their French. They become pupils at Mme Heger's pensionnat.

1843 Wordsworth becomes Poet Laureate.

1846 Emily's *Wuthering Heights*, Anne's *Agnes Grey* and Charlotte's *Jane Eyre* all published.

1848 Anne's *The Tenant of Wildfell Hall* published. Emily and

Branwell, the only brother, both die.

1849 Anne dies.

1850 *Shirley* published. Charlotte visits the Royal Academy and sees her hero, the Duke of Wellington. In this period she also meets William Thackeray and befriends Elizabeth Gaskell.

1852 Patrick's curate, Arthur Nicholls, proposes to Charlotte but her father forbids the match.

1853 *Villette* published.

1854 After a clandestine correspondence, Charlotte accepts Nicholls. They agree to stay with her father and marry in June.

1855 Charlotte dies, probably of pneumonia but there may also have been complications with a pregnancy. Patrick asks Elizabeth Gaskell, to write her biography.

1857 Gaskell's *Life of Charlotte Brontë* published.

1859 Patrick dies, aged 85, and Nicholls finally moves back to Ireland, where he remarries.

FURTHER READING

Allott, Miriam (ed), *Charlotte Brontë, Jane Eyre and Villette: A Casebook, Macmillan, 1973.*

Allott, Miriam (ed), *The Brontës: The Critical Heritage*, Routledge and Kegan Paul, 1974.

Barker, Juliet, *The Brontës, Weidenfeld and Nicolson,* 1994.

Bloom, Harold (ed), *Modern Critical Views: The Brontës*, Chelsea House Publishers, 1987.

Chase, Karen, Eros and Psyche: *The Representation of Personality in Charlotte Brontë, Charles Dickens, George Eliot,* Methuen, 1984.

Coveney, Peter, *The Image of Childhood, Penguin Books,* 1967.

Eagleton, *Terry, Myths of Power: A Marxist Study of the Brontës,* Macmillan, 1975.

Ewbank, Inga Stina, *Their Proper Sphere: A Study of the Brontë Sisters as Early-Victorian Female Novelists*, Edward Arnold, 1966.

Gaskell, Elizabeth, *The Life of Charlotte Brontë* (1855), Oxford World's Classics, 1996.

Gilbert, Sandra M. and Susan Gubar, *The Madwoman in the Attic and the Nineteenth-Century Literary Imagination*, Yale University Press, 1979.

Heilman, Robert B., 'Charlotte Brontë, Reason and the Moon', *Nineteenth-Century Fiction, XIV* (1960), 283-302.

Hughes, Kathryn, *The Victorian Governess*, The Hambledon Press, 1993.

Jackson, Rosemary, *The Literature of Subversion*, Routledge, 1981.

King, Jeanette, *Jane Eyre: Open Guides to Literature,* Open University Press, 1986.

Kroeber, Karl, *Styles in Fictional Structure: The Art of Jane Austen, Charlotte Brontë, George Eliot*, Princeton University Press, 1971.

Lodge, David, *The Language of Fiction: Essays In Criticism and Verbal Analysis of the English Novel*, Routledge and Kegan Paul, 1966.

Martin, Robert B., *The Accents of Persuasion*, Norton, 1966.

Maynard, John, *Charlotte Brontë and Sexuality*, Cambridge University Press, 1987.

Moglen, Helène, *Charlotte Brontë: The Self Conceived*, University of Wisconsin Press, 1984.

Poovey, Mary, *Uneven Developments: The Ideological Work of Gender in Mid-Victorian England,* University of Chicago Press, 1988.

Rich, Adrienne, *On Lies, Secrets, and Silence: Selected Prose 1966-1978*, W. W. Norton & Co, 1995.

Showalter, Elaine, *A Literature of Their Own: from Charlotte Brontë to Doris Lessing*, Princeton University Press, 1977.

Shuttleworth, Sally, *Charlotte Brontë and Victorian Psychology,* Cambridge University Press, 1996.

Shuttleworth, Sally, *The Mind of the Child, Child Development in Literature, Science, and Medicine, 1840-1900*, Oxford University Press, 2010.

Spivak, Gayatri Chakravorty, 'Three Women's Texts and a Critique of Imperialism', *Critical Inquiry*, University of Chicago Press, 1985.

Thormählen, Marianne, *The Brontës and Education,* Cambridge University Press, 2007.

Tillotson, Kathleen, *Novels of the Eighteen-Forties*, Oxford University Press, 1954.

INDEX

First published in 2014 by
Connell Guides
Artist House
35 Little Russell Street
London WC1A 2HH

10 9 8 7 6 5 4 3 2 1

Picture credits:
p.19 © Photos 12/Alamy
p.49 © Snap Stills/REX
p.59 © Archive Photos/Getty
p.73 © Paula Rego, *Biting* – Courtesy of Marlborough Fine Art, London
p.85 © c.Focus/Everett/REX
p.99 © Look and Learn/The Bridgeman Art Library/Private Collection -
Jane Eyre, English School, (20th century)
p.115 © Moviestore collection Ltd/Alamy

A CIP catalogue record for this book is available from the British Library.
ISBN 978-1-907776-17-5

Design © Nathan Burton
Assistant Editors:
Katie Sanderson, Paul Woodward & Pierre Smith Khanna

Printed in Italy by LEGO

www.connellguides.com